Undiscovered Victoria

A local's guide to finding adventure

From the team at
One Hour Out

Hardie Grant
EXPLORE

WELCOME TO COUNTRY

We acknowledge that we walk and travel on land that is not ours and we celebrate the First Nation Peoples' enduring love and ongoing connection to Country. We pay our respects to Elders past and present.

Always was. Always will be.

—

This book is dedicated to the people of Victoria, who consistently demonstrate community spirit, kindness and resilience in the face of all manner of adversity.

Contents

A TRAVEL GUIDE BORN
FROM STAYING AT HOME — IV
ONE HOUR OUT — VII
MAP OF VICTORIA — VIII
TRAVELLING TIPS — XI
HOW WE TRAVEL — XIV

Where we walk the water's edge
XVIII

Where we shop
30

Where they farm
60

Where we art
94

Where we get close to nature
132

Where we eat
164

Where we drink
188

INDEX — 216
PHOTOGRAPHY CREDITS — 221

A travel guide born from staying home

The seeds for this book were sown when the One Hour Out team – and millions of Melburnians – found ourselves in the unusual circumstance of being confined to our homes for a period of time (262 days to be exact!). The lockdowns introduced to curb the spread of Covid-19 meant all planned road trips were cancelled and along with the plans, all the joys of regional travel. No more plunging into the frigid waters of a favourite swimming hole, no chance to strike up conversations with outrageously fun hospo people and no hikes into national parks or across rocky coastal headlands. Indeed, for a while there, putting the bins out each week was considered quite the outdoor adventure, a trip to the supermarket as exhilarating (and at times dangerous) as hiking the Falls to Hotham Alpine Crossing in a snowstorm.

It was through this experience of being confined to our homes that we learned how much travel contributes to our lives. How much we benefit from the break from our daily routines, the chance to take in new vistas, to connect with new people or in a different way to our everyday people. We eagerly anticipated the chance to swap emails for gin tastings, vacuuming for window shopping and to swap school runs for beach walks.

Finally, during the summer of 2021-22, the worst of the pandemic had passed, and Victorians were able to travel once again. And boy, did we make the most of it. With international flights off the table, we kept it local, filling caravan parks, free-camping spots, Airbnbs and hotels across the state. Second-hand campertrailers were snapped up in minutes, retailers of camping equipment struggled with demand and an order for a new motorhome could take 12 months for delivery.

Victorians have always been great travellers within their own state, but now a renewed interest in our local surroundings appeared. Suddenly we were inspired to look inwards, within our own state, our own community, our own natural environment, the towns, the villages, the local watering holes and indeed, within ourselves.

Being locked together as a community created a desire to connect with that same community. It awakened within us a desire to stay local and reconsider how well we know our own backyard. Suddenly a 10-day package deal to Phuket didn't have the same appeal. Instead, a three-day canoeing trip down in the south-west of Victoria (*see* p. 25), paddling through the mist rising against the limestone cliffs as birds darted to and fro from their nests sounded far more appealing.

Instead of planning out a long and expensive trip to Europe with dreams of browsing the great departments stores of Milan or Zurich, we now craved a weekend in a rural town like Kyneton where one might stumble across an old pub (*see* p. 39) that has been completely refitted as a multi-level department store, including a stunning cocktail bar and Raffles-inspired verandah seating.

Or perhaps instead of booking flights to a country in the Middle East for a motor sport, we instead might make plans to take a drive up the Hume Highway to seek out one of the world's largest collections of motor vehicles (*see* p. 123) in Shepparton, featuring the full gamut of combustion classics from a sleek '65 T-bird that somehow found its way here from LA, to a collection of Harleys that would bring the most hardened bikie to tears.

This book is for the local explorer. For the curious mind willing to dig a little deeper into the familiar. Those who find joy in the small and seemingly insignificant. Those who are willing to take the time to drive the backroads, stop at roadside stalls, pull up a stool in a country pub, check out the local swimming hole and walk to the top of a hill, just to see what's there. Whether you want to meet makers or producers, have a cultural experience with Traditional Owners or simply drive to a dining destination for an amazing meal, *Undiscovered Victoria* has you covered.

The team at One Hour Out has covered a hell of a lot of kilometres in the production of this book, to every corner of the state and, yet, we feel as if we've only scratched the surface. There are plenty of roads we didn't get to travel down and galleries and restaurants we will have to get to another time. Our journeys have further opened our eyes to the depth and quality of experiences that make Victoria such an admirable travel destination. You will find each place included has an indication of distance from Melbourne/Naarm – whether one hour out or two or three – or more – and we encourage you to keep exploring a little further and further.

We hope the places we have picked for this book bring you lots of joy and some crazy adventures but, more importantly, we hope the book becomes a catalyst for you to discover your own Undiscovered Victoria.

See you on the road.

Jay Dillon
Founder – One Hour Out

TOP Jay Dillon BOTTOM LEFT Richard Cornish BOTTOM RIGHT Dellaram Vreeland

ONEHOUROUT.COM.AU

One Hour Out

One Hour Out is an online publication dedicated to promoting all the best things from outside the city. We celebrate regional communities and champion their creativity, innovation and resilience. We encourage our city cousins to come respectfully explore the landscapes of country Victoria and connect with the people who call it home.

JAY DILLON

Jay Dillon grew up in the small coastal town of Batemans Bay on the South Coast of NSW, where he donned a satin blue bow tie and cummerbund in his first job at Raymond's Chinese Restaurant (featured in the ABC series *Chopsticks or Fork?*). This was the start of a 15-year career in hospitality, which strangely involved a degree in contemporary visual arts, a career in digital media and a dalliance with the bottled water industry when he launched the award-winning brand Another Bloody Water with two friends in 2010. Despite a short stint testing out life in the inner suburbs of Melbourne, Jay has always lived and worked in regional areas and is passionate about championing regional businesses and communities. Since moving to the Yarra Valley, Jay has been deeply involved with regional small businesses and has a passion for sustainable tourism. In 2018, Jay launched One Hour Out, after observing a lack of coverage of hospitality, cultural and nature-based experiences in regional areas. In this capacity, Jay takes every opportunity to hit the road (with two somewhat reluctant teenagers in tow) to explore the incredibly rich landscape and fascinating characters throughout Victoria.

RICHARD CORNISH

Richard Cornish has written about regional Victoria since he started writing more than 30 years ago. Having grown up in the bush he has a keen understanding of the natural environment. He also has a deep grasp of the importance of the built environment and how valuable cultural capital is to communities. For almost a decade he travelled to every town and region in the state for the popular weekly column Six Reasons to Visit for the Saturday *Age*. Over that time Richard sought out the lesser-known, undiscovered, quirky and downright fascinating places that tourism offices overlook. Richard is best known as an award-winning food writer, co-author of the Movida book series and the man who has penned Good Food's Brain Food column for over ten years. He still writes about country, food and people and works with businesses to help them tell their stories. He lives in St Kilda with his family, large productive garden and two dogs.

DELLARAM VREELAND

Dellaram Vreeland proclaims herself to be regional Victoria's strongest advocate. Growing up in Ballarat, she's spent her life touring the villages and hamlets scattered across the state, eager to discover the glistening pearls that lie hidden within. As a journalist, she's spent a good part of the last decade uncovering the stories behind the people and places who inject beauty and awe into their surrounding communities. Covering everything from arts to culture, travel to multicultural affairs, Dellaram's work has appeared in the *Guardian Australia*, across various Nine and Australian Community Media mastheads, as well as in a variety of print and online publications that promote the wonders of regional Australia including *Pandaemonium*, Historic Stays and, of course, One Hour Out. She is the founder of online magazine *Jamál* which is dedicated to showcasing regional Australia's diverse and evolving cultural landscape. Her days are spent tending to her family of five while striving her best to contribute to the vibrancy of her own community in Ballarat, which she dotes upon so very much.

ADDITIONAL CONTRIBUTIONS

We would like to thank the following writers from One Hour Out whose contributions often made it into this book:

Mike Emmett
Anthea Riskas
Mandy Kennedy
Gwen O'Toole
Tehya Nicholas

Thank you to Faye McCormack for holding the One Hour Out fort during this period of researching and writing a book.

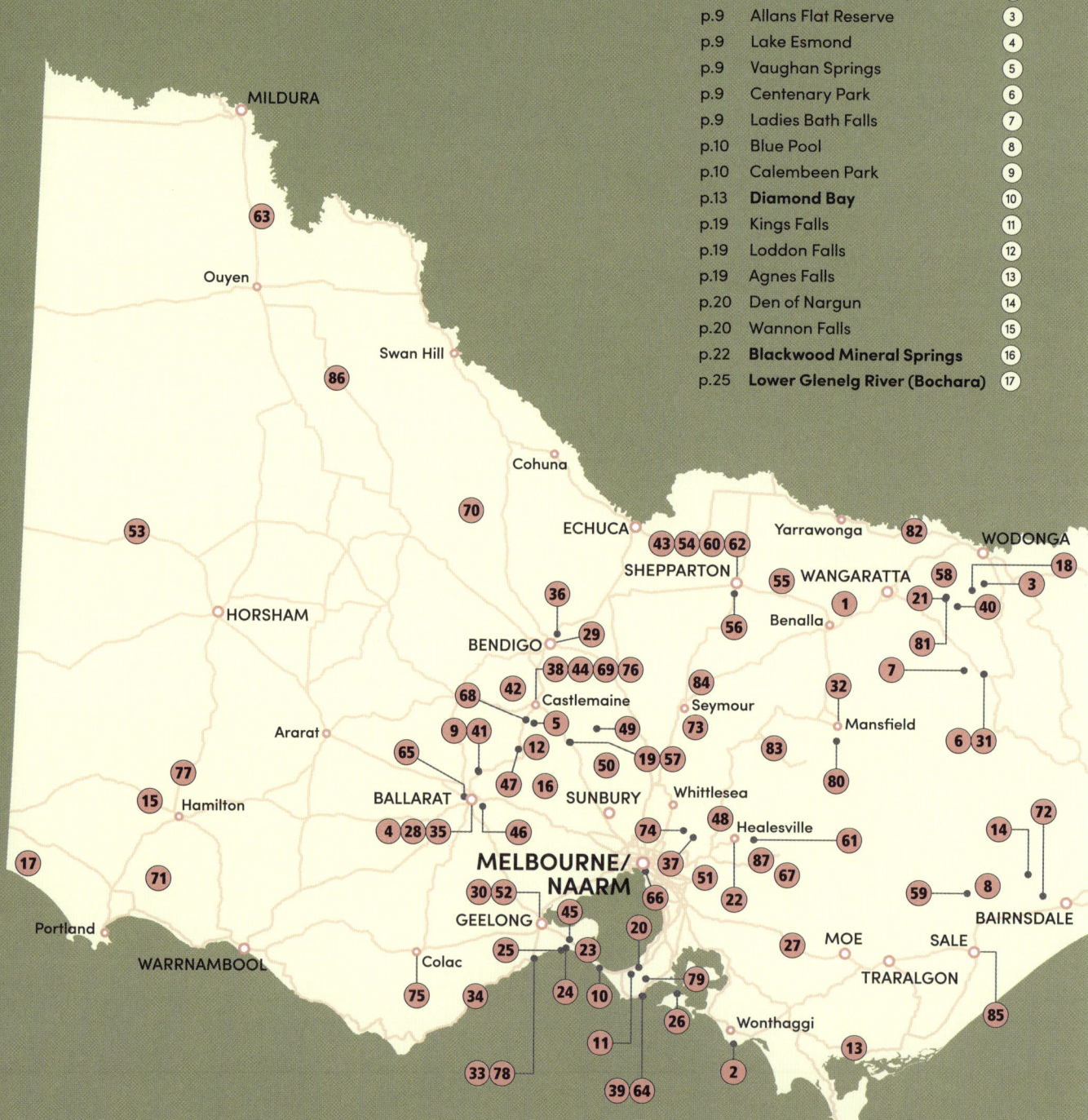

Where we shop

p.34	Feather & Drum Custom Hat Co.	18
p.39	Royal George Hotel	19
p.42	Dromana Habitat	20
p.46	Beechworth Conservatory	21
p.49	Verso Books	22
p.49	The Bookshop at Queenscliff	23
p.49	Bookgrove	24
p.49	Heads and Tales Bookstore	25
p.50	Turn the Page Bookshop	26
p.50	Need2Read	27
p.50	The Known World	28
p.50	Bendigo Book Mark	29
p.50	The Book Bird	30
p.50	The Bright Bookshop	31
p.50	Ink Bookshop	32
p.50	Torquay Books	33
p.50	Lorne Books	34
p.52	Windflower	35
p.57	Bendigo Antiques and Collectibles Centre	36

Where they farm

p.64	Gawa Wurundjeri Resource Trail	37
p.67	Long Paddock Cheese	38
p.70	Flinders Mussels	39
p.77	Black Barn Farm	40
p.82	Le Péché Gourmand	41
p.82	Maldon Bakery	42
p.82	Tinto	43
p.82	Johnny Baker	44
p.82	Ket Baker	45
p.84	Inglenook Dairy	46
p.87	Daylesford Longhouse	47
p.90	Edible Forest	48

Where we art

p.98	Pom-me-granite	49
p.102	Mount Monument	50
p.106	Chojo Feature Trees Gallery and Nursery	51
p.109	Boom Gallery	52
p.112	Australian Pinball Museum	53
p.117	Shepparton Art Museum	54
p.120	Secret Garden Gigs	55
p.123	MOVE	56
p.127	Stockroom	57
p.130	Yeddonba Aboriginal Cultural Site	58

Where we get close to nature

p.136	Wildflower spotting, Valencia Creek	59
p.140	The Flats, Mooroopna	60
p.142	Leadbeater's possum, Yarra Ranges	61
p.148	Australian Botanic Gardens	62
p.151	Hattah-Kulkyne National Park	63
p.154	Weedy sea dragons, Flinders Pier	64
p.157	Ballarat's Avenue of Honour	65
p.157	River red gum	66
p.157	Ada Tree	67
p.158	The Big Tree	68
p.158	The English oak	69
p.158	Scar Tree, Boort	70
p.161	Budj Bim Cultural Landscape	71

Where we eat

p.168	The Long Paddock	72
p.171	Trawool Estate	73
p.174	Greasy Zoe's	74
p.177	Babil at Oddfellows	75
p.180	Bar Midland	76
p.183	Bunyip Hotel	77
p.186	Mortadeli	78

Where we drink

p.192	Kerri Greens	79
p.197	Swiftcrest Distillery	80
p.200	Billson's Brewery and the Soda Bar	81
p.204	Chambers Rosewood Winery	82
p.209	The Alexandra Hotel	83
p.209	Harvest Home	84
p.210	Criterion Hotel	85
p.210	Royal Hotel, Sea Lake	86
p.212	Silva Coffee	87

Corryong

Orbost

Travelling tips

To travel in Victoria is to travel without fear of any of the potential dangers that you might find in other parts of the world. The chances of being kidnapped, imprisoned or eaten alive by an apex predator are extremely remote, so long as you stick to the track and proudly announce your football team when entering the front bar.

Below are our top tips for a safe and comfortable road trip across Victoria. Some are for basic survival and others are just to keep the peace with those travelling with you and the people you meet along the way. They are formed from years of travelling around Victoria via various transport modes and with a various mix of passenger types, from a full family frolic that includes a newborn time-bomb, to a carefree carload of festival-seeking mates, to a podcast-listening, daydream-inducing solo jaunt.

We hope you find some fresh ideas for improving your own road trip adventures.

A PRE-DEPARTURE ZHUZH

As if getting packed to leave isn't time-consuming enough, seriously though, this is one of those level-A pro-tips that will bring so much joy when you arrive back home totally depleted and with barely enough energy to dial pizza delivery.

Even if it's just stacking the dishwasher and throwing the doona on the bed, making your home a little tidier – or stylish – for when you arrive back can make all the difference. Better yet, have a meal cooked and in the fridge or freezer for when you arrive home – especially after a long weekend away. There've been times for us where this sort of delayed gratification was the highlight of the trip!

GET THE WORM

The sun peeking over the horizon, sleepy passengers snuggled in the back, just you and the odd tradie making the most of an empty highway. This is what early road trip starts are made of. Not only will you beat the rush-hour traffic, but there's something about a super-early start that renders the anguish of a long drive to a gratefully inaccessible part of the subconscious. Plus you've gone and got yourself at least an extra half-day of jovial holiday activities with your loved ones (and a good excuse for an afternoon hammock nap!).

BECOME A MASTER OF YOUR GPS APP

Nothing has had a bigger effect on travel than GPS mapping apps. In the lead-up to any trip, we always create a new list and pin each of the key locations of our itinerary and then make sure to download this map so that it is available offline. There will be times where you find yourself lost in a mobile blackspot, and this simple trick will save your bacon many times over.

DIRECTIONS ARE NEVER TO BE DISCUSSED

We are hesitant to turn this into a guide for healthy relationships, but we recommend that once the directions are set on the app, no further discussion should be entered into. Sure, there may be the odd recommendation to take a dirt road when there is a perfectly good highway running alongside, but that's much better than the vague directions from a co-passenger who once holidayed here as a child.

DON'T FORGET THE LITTLE PEOPLE

Speaking of children – if you want to put pause to the incessant 'are we there yet?' question from the little ones, pull up a GPS app on a separate phone for them to follow along with. It's also smart to help them pack together a fun box, filled with colouring-in books, small toys and plenty of snacks! The ABC Listen app has a whole section dedicated to kids with lots of stories, music and games.

We find that the older ones just need a reminder to download shows and music the night before we leave and to make sure their devices (and any batteries) are charged, and cords and power adapters are packed.

The whole trip shouldn't be a private experience though, so we like to make time for group activities and games at stages throughout the trip. 'Car cricket' is a favourite (the person 'batting' gets a single 'run' for a white car, four 'runs' for a caravan and a six for bus). On a quiet country road we play 'Hey cow', which involves briefly stopping to yell out 'Hey cow' to a herd and counting how many look our way!

PACK FOR SOMETHING TO GO WRONG

The irony of Murphy's law is that the list of things that can go wrong includes no one remembering who was the originator of the popular adage. Regardless, it's an important lesson for preparing for a road trip as you never know when the poo will flick up and hit the fan-belt. Here's a few things we like to keep in the car, just in case it does:

- Plenty of water – a bottle for each passenger and one for the car.
- Spare tyre – we all know we have one somewhere, but is it pumped up and do you know how to get it out (and fit it)?
- Jumper leads – be sure to check your owner's manual before using them; you might only need them once in a blue moon, but you will always be grateful they are there.
- A warm jumper or coat – our one is dusty and unloved, jammed under the driver's seat, however it has made bearable many unexpected late-night emergencies.
- A first-aid kit – with a few basics like band-aids, bandages and paracetamol.
- Wildlife rescue kit – we recommend a blanket or pillow case for wrapping up any injured wildlife that might need care. A pair of leather gardening gloves to protect yourself from scratches is also worth having stored away. A list of local wildlife refuge locations can be found on the Victorian Government website (wildlife.vic.gov.au).
- Spare car key – pop it into a bag that is often taken with a passenger (handbags are perfect).
- Roadside assistance account – whether taken up through your car warranty or as a yearly fee with the RACV (racv.com.au), those angels will get you back on the road in a jiffy.
- A notepad and pen – to jot down important details such as the address and key code for accommodation (just in case we can't access these details with our devices when we need to).
- Spare cash – for those odd times where it's cash only (e.g. farm gates) or the terminal is down.
- Phone charger and cords.

GIVE THE HEADS-UP

Many are the lost hikers who could have saved themselves a terrifying night in the bush by letting someone know of their plans. By giving someone you trust the details of your itinerary and sharing the previously downloaded map, you are giving yourself the best chance for a quick extraction should the alarm need to be sounded. If you are actually going bush and hiking or camping solo, a Personal Locator Beacon (PLB) can also be a lifesaver.

PLAN AHEAD

In these post-pandemic times, it's worth considering booking ahead for some activities such as tours and high-end dining experiences. Many venues now operate on reduced hours and limited seating capacity in order to accommodate a limited pool of hospitality staff (and for the sake of the owners' sanity). We'd hate for you to miss out on any of the special experiences listed in this book due to there being no spots available, so a little pre-planning is a good idea.

DRIVER CHOOSES THE MUSIC

The driver gets to choose the music or podcast. There, that's final now. No correspondence will be entered into. And if said driver happens to be a die-hard fan of German grind metal … well, everyone else can just get themselves headphones. Besides, other passengers have the option of watching a movie or even reading a book if their vestibular system is rigorous enough.

ROADSIDE SHOPPING

Just like in life generally, it's always worth taking the time to enjoy the journey as much as the destination itself. One way that we have leaned into this notion is to be willing to stop at roadside stalls or farm gates. Sometimes they appear as quaint little timber boxes with an honesty box next to a gate or a collection of fruit-laden trestle tables that finally reveal themselves after a long line of quirky hand-written signs on the side of the road. Either way, they quite often contain high-quality seasonal produce straight off the farm, with the added bonus of providing farmers an income that circumvents the hard bargaining of supermarket buyers.

Plus, the chance to to show kids where their food comes from and then look in the rearview mirror and see smiling faces smothered in figs and berries is one of life's joys.

THE POWER OF POWER NAPS

Power naps are amazing, they truly are. We've napped in small town parks, besides rivers and creeks and alongside smelly supermarket skips. All it takes is a 10min snooze stretched out on the back seat to feel totally refreshed and ready to hit the road again. In the meantime, the other passengers can go off on some type of adventure that usually results in an amusing encounter with nature or a soft-serve ice-cream. It's getting to the point where roadside naps are a highlight for our travels!

THE FUEL OLYMPICS

The changeover from petrol to electric vehicles is surely one of the most exciting changes to travel that's underway right now, and a change we are eager to make ourselves – not just for the sake of the environment, but for the health of our back pocket too. In the meantime, we play cat-and-mouse with the petroleum companies who seem to have the single-minded goal of extracting as much money from us as possible. There are some great apps out there that will guide you towards the cheapest fuel option around you. Country servos are usually more expensive than their city counterparts, so we love some of the apps that will guide you towards the cheapest fuel option. Some apps from servo brands even let you lock in the cheaper fuel price from the city that you can then utilise at their other country outlets. There are always new ways to find the cheapest way to keep the car running, so let's keep on fighting the good fight until we can all go electric!

GET YOUR BEARINGS

Once the bags are in and the battle of the beds is complete, we like to put on a coat (and beanie in winter) and head out to see what's around. There's nothing like a few laps around the block to get your bearings and we usually get the best 'insider' information into what's happening in the community by talking with staff at the local cafe, pub or newsagency. The local informants always seem to have their finger on the pulse as to the most spectacular hiking spots, who the young gun winemakers are and where to get the best vanilla slice.

THE PATIENCE OF BUDDHA

The mysterious disappearance of hospitality workers since the pandemic has also resulted in a challenge for venues to deliver the high standard of service that was once the standard. This simply requires a big scoop of patience topped with a little bit of empathy and served with an appreciation for how lucky we are to be free to explore and connect with the passionate people and inspirational places of Victoria.

DON'T LEAVE FOR HOME TOO LATE

Depending on where you are coming from, we recommend not leaving it too late to start the drive home – especially if you're travelling on a weekend, a public holiday or at the end of a school holiday period. Everyone has the same plan of trying to get in a full day of activities on the last days and then leaving late afternoon. A post-holiday traffic jam is most certainly the roughest reality re-entry. If you are not in the position to stay an extra day or two, consider leaving before lunch, which not only means you will miss holidaymaker queues, but you'll be back with lots of time to unpack and prepare for the week ahead.

STRAIGHT TO THE LAUNDRY

Do not pass go, do not collect sand in the bedroom. Our tip to ensure a smooth unpacking process that doesn't last for a full week is to implement a rule whereby each passenger must take their bag directly to the laundry for stage one processing. Here, the laundry functions more like the airlock of a level four biomedical laboratory, where all clothing materials must be decontaminated (i.e. put into the washing machine) before leaving the facility. After this, it's just a matter of putting away the other items and storing the bags away. Extra dessert for those who go back out to help bring in eskies, camping gear and other items. It's all about putting in the hard work upfront for maximum relaxation gains.

How we travel

'It's not the destination, **it's** the journey', is often quoted for inspiring others to take the time to enjoy life as they head towards their goals. We take a more literal translation when planning out our journey within this fine state.

Victoria is particularly well served with different ways to get around and we encourage you to experiment with a mode of transport that you might never think to choose. It's all about seeing things from a different perspective, at a different pace, via a different route.

CAR

Whether it's jostling for pole position on a four-lane highway, or avoiding pot holes on a country laneway, Victoria is predominantly made for car travel and we are not going to pretend otherwise.

Most journeys from Melbourne/Naarm involve one of the major highways, swiftly transporting you to within a bumpy backroad of your end destination. A coastal jaunt begins with the Princes Hwy, which takes you to the South Australia border via Geelong and the Great Ocean Road in one direction and through the heart of Gippsland into NSW in the other direction.

The Western Hwy will take you out to Ballarat, then to Gariwerd/Grampians and on to the Wimmera's endless crop fields. The Hume Fwy takes you straight up into the High Country with tempting diversions to the King Valley or Goulburn Valley. The Calder Hwy is a direct route to the thriving city of Bendigo and across the expansive Mallee farmlands to Mildura on the banks of the Murray River.

However, it's all in the timing. Pity the fool who decides to take a fully-loaded family wagon onto the Calder Fwy at 3pm on the Friday before the Labour Day long weekend. May the Lord have mercy on the ambitious driver who thinks leaving as soon as the kids get home from school will get them to their Airbnb in time to watch the sunset with a glass of sparkling in hand. These things require the strategic planning of a major military operation and a heavy dose of luck.

When you do arrive, the car is your ticket for really unearthing the hidden secrets of any region. We love to take the backroads of the countryside or purposely take the long way back to our home base. We can't count the amount of times we've happened across the cutest of villages or abundant fruit stands purely from ignoring the directions of the GPS and going off-piste. The willingness to go the long way around is the foundation for this book and we implore you to do the same.

CYCLING

We love the pace of cycling. Compared to walking, you really feel like you are getting somewhere at a rapid pace, with still enough time to take in the smaller details like the little critters that scramble along roadside embankments and duck into lakeside weeds. Details usually lost when zooming past in a car.

As a result of the pandemic lockdowns, just about every Victorian has a bicycle now, and by sheer luck we also have an abundance of places to ride them. We are particularly fond of the Victorian Rail Trail network that seems to grow each year. Trains have always been terrible at climbing hills and so us modern-day cycling families benefit from the gentle gradients, contoured hills and fantastic timber and steel bridges that were constructed in the heyday of train travel.

Of course, for some, that's not quite enough of a challenge and the more adventurous (and slightly insane) amongst us

are also well catered for. Mountain biking continues to grow in popularity in Australia, and Victoria is really coming to the party with more than 1300km of trails, from gravity-defying singletracks to flowing backcountry trails.

Large legs in lycra (also the name of our new band!) have plenty of opportunities to test their stamina, with the roads to ski resorts like Falls Creek, Mount Baw Baw and Mount Buffalo providing satisfactorily challenging hill climbs from spring to autumn.

WALKING

The pure variety of landscapes in this wonderful state make for some of the greatest walking adventures. The walks of Victoria possibly don't get the same attention as those in other states, which is fantastic for those that don't like to share a trail.

There are spectacular coastal walks in just about every section of our almost 2000km of coastline, which will see you traverse rocky outcrops, golden sandy shores and rugged cliff-top edges that overlook the grumpiest of seas. There are ridge-top trails across alpine mountains that can either be filled with a kaleidoscope of colour and the scent from wildflowers or shrouded in snow and ice amongst granite and snow gums in winter. Or there are delightful lakeside strolls, with river gums and reeds making a home to all varieties of waterfowl and amphibians.

Admittedly, we fit into the category of 'sometimes annoying people' who will always stop and read the information placed along a trail. These plaques often transport our minds back in time by laying out the First Nations culture or European history of an area, or leave our heads spinning with a geological explanation of how the landscape was formed across millions of years. We are always grateful to the councils or community groups who install and manage this information for the benefit of the passing walker.

For some people a good walk means to load up all the requirements for survival onto your back and set off for three to four nights of solid hill climbs and campfire dinners. For others it means a quick stroll around town, people watching and window shopping before happy hour. We are a little bit of both and take every chance we can to explore this fine state by foot.

XVI   UNDISCOVERED VICTORIA

TRAIN

People have long been captivated by the romance of train travel, from the mystery and luxury of the *Orient Express* carting Parisian adventurers to Venice or Istanbul, to the incredible engineering feat of Switzerland's *Glacier Express* that conquers the ice-capped mountains between St Moritz and Zermatt. Now, we aren't suggesting the V/Line from Melbourne to Kerang should be held with the same reverence, but still there are some good reasons for making use of Victoria's regional train network.

At the time of writing, the state government has introduced a regional fare cap, so you can now travel to any part of Victoria for $10. Considering a tank of petrol these days requires a small bank loan, it's a significantly cheaper transport option (at least for those still burning fossil fuels), and by avoiding peak-hour traffic, travel time is about the same as taking to the road. Add to this the ability to sit back, read a book, play some cards or just gaze out the window in half a dream while you are swiftly transported to your destination, then it's an option worthy of consideration. Most of the V/Line network carriages include a food and drink cart too. It might not be up there with the fine-dining experience of *The Ghan*, but sometimes a meat pie and sauce is exactly what is required after a long weekend of hiking and wine tasting.

Another benefit of train travel is that it involves getting up close with some of the grandest historical structures in Victoria. A railway trip to Maryborough, for example, is well worth it just for the chance to stroll through the 19th-century ornate station, and on a trip to Malmsbury you will cross the Malmsbury viaduct, which was once Australia's tallest stone bridge.

Yes, sir, trains can indeed get you to your destination, but they can also provide you with an experience as well. There are some wonderful steam train experiences throughout Victoria, where you and the family have the opportunity to take in the scenery in a manner befitting another era. *Puffing Billy* that climbs its way through the Dandenong Ranges and the Bellarine Railway in Queenscliff with the exceptionally fun *Blues Train* are both well-known examples, however with a little more digging it's possible to enjoy the joys of train travel almost everywhere. Visitors to Mildura can take a ride on the cute-as-a-button *Lukee* from the equally cute Red Cliffs Historical Steam Railway, whilst in the glorious village of Walhalla you can have the option to peer out across the Thomas River as the *Fowler* diesel locomotive crosses six large trestle bridges.

FERRY

For some reason Victoria's ferry network doesn't get talked about as a fine way for travelling throughout Victoria. Many are familiar with the Sorrento to Queenscliff trip which connects two of our most famous food and wine regions – the Mornington and Bellarine peninsulas – however there are other boat rides connecting delightful destinations that are waiting for you to explore.

In addition to the aforementioned Sorrento to Queenscliff ferry, Searoad Ferries manages a 400-person catamaran inside Western Port that links the Mornington Peninsula (Stony Point jetty) with Phillip Island and French Island, where you can connect with a tour company that will take you to each of the historic sites and go searching for wildlife.

Port Phillip Ferries has a new terminal at Docklands in Melbourne/Naarm and regularly teams up with Bellarine Peninsula businesses like Jack Rabbit Winery and *The Q Train* rail restaurant for spectacular full-day experiences of food, wine and travel. They also run a service to Geelong and a Footy Ferry service that links fans between Geelong stadium and the MCG and Docklands.

Then there are the small practical ferry trips that still have their own special charm, like the car punt from Paynesville to Raymond Island with its abundance of wild koalas and lakeside picnic spots. Or taking your vehicle aboard the last two ferries that cross the Murray River: the *Spirit of Wymah* at Granya and the *Speewa Ferry* north of Swan Hill.

TRAVELLING SUSTAINABLY

We know 'sustainable travel' is a term thrown around a lot lately; for us it just means taking the time to slow down and give some consideration to the impact that we might have on any environment that we enter.

For us that starts with how we pack, ensuring that everything we bring is reusable and anything that isn't reusable (e.g. packaging) we take back with us again and recycle.

We are also big believers in the saying that 'every dollar you spend is a vote for the world you want to live in', and as much as possible we try to spend our money within the local community itself. This might mean choosing to eat at small locally owned cafes and restaurants rather than multinational chains, as well as making sure we head home with an esky filled with goodies made by local producers.

We are conscious of how short-term accommodation is reducing housing options for local people in many regions and will tend to make use of local caravan parks and hotels instead.

We also give consideration to our impact on the natural environment by sticking to the walking tracks, only setting up camp on allocated campsites, bringing in our own firewood and giving wildlife a clear berth when we do cross paths.

Together these actions ensure that our travels leave a positive impact on the communities we visit and natural environment, contributing to the long-term sustainability of both.

Where we walk the water's edge

There's no denying Victoria is renowned for being home to some of the most sublime beaches in the world. People travel from near and far to venture along the Great Ocean Road, to Phillip Island and the Mornington Peninsula – their pristine shores, blue waters and holiday towns beckon one and all. We're all well aware of the beauty afforded by the likes of Torquay, Lorne, Apollo Bay, Sorrento and those fluffy little penguins at Phillip Island. But if you ask us (which you are), we prefer to avoid the horde of tourists who make a beeline for the tried and true, and instead head to some of the lesser-known alcoves that offer seaside serenity sans crowds. We've come up with a list of some of Victoria's more elusive beaches, so you can plan your own peaceful beachside getaways.

Then there are those of us who prefer riversides to ocean tides. Who enjoy surrounding ourselves with verdant and native forests as we frolic the afternoon away in lovely lakes and babbling brooks. Take for instance the hideaway of Blackwood Mineral Springs (*see* p.22), with its dense Australian bushland, rivers and lagoons, perfect for freshening up on a hot summer's day. Or the expansive Winton Wetlands (*see* p.4) that are not only a case study in wetland regeneration, but also offers visitors the chance to find out about Traditional culture through the Lotjpatj Natjan Danak sculpture trail.

Whenever we travel across this vast state, we can't help but feel an overwhelming sense of appreciation to the Traditional Owners, who for tens of thousands of years cared for the rivers and seas (and entire land), and continue to treat the waterways, inlets and shores with respect and love. Were it not for their enduring care for Country, we wouldn't all be able to experience the bountiful oceans and riverways as we do today.

So whether it's the beach you seek, or the stream which you yearn for, it's important to look around you, remember those who came before you and those who are to come after you, and treat the stunning land with the same amount of respect as the Traditional Owners have always shown. Let's keep Victoria's rivers and seas the most talked about in the world.

Let's go swimming!

#TWOANDAHALFHOURSOUT

Winton Wetlands

DELLARAM VREELAND

There are many magnificent natural sites scattered across our vast and varied state with such rich stories to tell from the past, the present and even the future. If only there were ways we could unearth all those tales and discover more about how these places came to be.

Located between Benalla and Wangaratta on Yorta Yorta Country, the Winton Wetlands is a place that shares those stories. An all-encompassing destination, the wetlands not only sate our desire to connect with nature, but also enrich our understanding of the local area and its Traditional Owners.

Dubbed the largest restoration project in the southern hemisphere, the wetlands' collaborators are on a mission to renew the ecology of the reserve and grow its natural, scientific, cultural and environmental significance. There's a huge emphasis on education here and the visitor experience incorporates recreation, tourism and community development. Wherever you are at the wetlands, you'll find that the entire space has been curated to enable this.

The sheer expanse of the area means there is much to explore and it's easy to spend a day here. Your first stop should be the Welcome Trail with its information on the wetlands, the local flora and fauna and historical anecdotes. The Lotjpatj Natjan Danak sculpture trail is a not-to-be-missed immersive creation of works created by 15 Yorta Yorta artists representing their living culture and it's really rather profound to interact with their stories through art.

The abundant wildlife here makes it really special too, and you'll spot free-roaming kangaroos, lizards and various birds – just a few of the animals we met during our visit.

You can choose to venture here for the day, but we recommend packing your camping gear and bicycles and setting up base for a couple of nights or more. Stargaze in the clear, unobstructed north-eastern skies, wake to the sound of birdsong, admire the

WHERE WE WALK THE WATER'S EDGE

natural Australian bushland, take a sunrise stroll along one of a series of walking tracks, or simply sit back and soak up the tranquillity that an escape from the hustle and bustle provides. Just a note: the camping sites don't have shower facilities, so make sure you're all scrubbed up prior to your escape.

The wetlands also feature their own Hub, playground and cafe, so you won't need to go without your caffeine fix. If you're here for the day, you can start your experience with a decent dose of locally sourced brekky (the menu boasts everything from classic smashed avo to wholesome breakfast bowls), or round off your wetlands exploration with a hearty lunch – think gnocchi with slow-cooked lamb, pumpkin arancini, fish and chips or handmade zucchini fritters. All cafe proceeds go towards further environmental restoration of the wetlands site, which is yet another bonus of dining out here.

It's not often we think of wetlands as a tourist attraction, but whether you want to walk, cycle, birdwatch, camp or just relax, the Winton Wetlands will give you an appreciation for history, culture, science and nature.

WETLANDS TO WATERCOLOUR

On your way to or from the wetlands, make sure to make a pit stop at the iconic **Benalla Art Gallery**. Nestled within the Benalla Botanical Gardens, the gallery's art collection spans three centuries of Australian art, from the early 19th century to the present day, as well as an impressive range of Traditional and contemporary First Nations artworks and modern and contemporary pieces from the 20th and 21st centuries. Admire the permanent collection, visit the travelling exhibitions, explore the public programs, then settle in for a nice coffee and cake at the on-site cafe.

Swimming holes

DELLARAM VREELAND

There's something so magical about whiling a long summer day away in a secluded rockpool surrounded by the great Australian bush, and the good news is experiences like this don't require a flight to the tropical north. Swimming pools and beaches are great and all, but we certainly love sporting our finest swimwear (whether you call them togs, bathers or cossies) and hitting up Victoria's natural swimming holes and all their accompanying wonders. We've rounded up a few of our faves for your perusal.

#TWOHOURSOUT
Cape Paterson Rockpool

Discover a state of pure calm as you sport your finest budgie smugglers and bathe the day away in the large rockpool of Cape Paterson Bay. Cloaked in tones of turquoise and teal, this built structure was blasted with dynamite in the 1960s but remains one of the most popular places to visit along the Bass Coast. The pool boasts both a deep end and a shallow end, making it the perfect summer swim spot for all ages. And even if you're not up for a dip, the surrounding beaches are also hotspots for fishing, diving and surfing.

#THREEANDAHALFHOURSOUT
Allans Flat Reserve

Created during the gold-rush days from dredge mining, the Allans Flat Reserve lake is a popular swimming spot for locals located 8km from Yackandandah. Pack your picnic and swimming gear (you will need a licence if you plan to fish) and enjoy a nice cool swim during the warm summer days and evenings, admiring the beautiful High Country sunsets and mountainous backdrop. Just note that the entrance to the reserve is on an unmade road and easy to miss, so make sure to keep an eye on the turn-off to Allans Flat Rd.

OPPOSITE Lake Esmond

#ONEANDAHALFHOURSOUT
Lake Esmond

Ballarat is renowned for the popular attraction of Sovereign Hill but there's a swimming destination nearby that's one of those elusive spots that only the locals know about. Originally a quarry for the local Eureka Tile Works until 1982, Lake Esmond was replanted and revived as a lake and reserve. Offering an all-in-one experience, the lake is not only a peaceful place to cool off on a hot day, but includes an ascent to a fabulous playground with toilets and barbecue and picnic facilities, lots of shaded areas, an expansive green space perfect for team sports, and walking trails through the lush native landscape.

#ONEANDAHALFHOURSOUT
Vaughan Springs

Our family loves visiting this swimming hole and campground located between Daylesford and Castlemaine on the banks of the Loddon River. The riverbank here is a beautiful place to spend the summer season or just visit for a daytrip if you're exploring the nearby towns. The paddle pool sits at the base of a steep, rugged cliff with lush, towering trees providing shade and picturesque surrounds. Also boasting a huge metal slide, mineral springs, ample parking (perfect for the kids to ride around on their scooters!), barbecue and picnic facilities and lots of walking tracks, there's plenty more to do here than just take a dip. Check ahead with Parks Victoria before visiting as the area was impacted by flooding in late 2022.

#FOURHOURSOUT
Centenary Park

Situated on the Ovens River in the holiday town of Bright in the High Country, this natural swimming pool has a lot going for it. Providing endless hours of summer fun (thanks also to the addition of a free splash park, playground and picnic facilities), the entire space does wonders for imbuing a sense of relaxation. Picnic tables line the grassy riverbank, river red gums provide lush canopies, toddlers paddle in the pebbled creek and families set up base as they await the golden sunset.

#FOURHOURSOUT
Ladies Bath Falls

There's a reason behind the name of these falls, located in the midst of Mount Buffalo National Park. In the early 20th century, travellers would stop here to cool off on their way to the Mount Buffalo chalet. The men and women would separate and the women would dip their toes in the refreshing Crystal Brook waters. You'll see water cascading into a beautifully clear pool, perfect to escape the summer heat. Just be careful when you're cooling off because the rocks can be quite slippery. While you're here, have a look at the chalet itself – you can't go in but you can peer in the windows and see a time-capsule of a bygone era of guest houses. It's also worth noting to check the Parks Victoria website (parks.vic.gov.au) prior to visiting so you're up to date with any walking track or road closures or changed conditions.

#THREEHOURSOUT
Blue Pool

A waterhole and gorge near Briagolong in Gippsland, Blue Pool is a fave among the locals with a towering bluff that overlooks the entire area. The natural pool consists of a large shallow waterhole that quickly deepens, and swimmers love jumping off the nearby cliff or the epic rope. (There are serious risks with this though and if you decide to do it, make sure you check the depth and exactly where the rocks are before jumping.) When the sun hits just right, the pool turns a magical blue, hence its name. It also features some fab walking trails that meander through the great Aussie bush, free campsites and barbecue facilities. It's a lovely place to while away a lazy summer's day with loved ones. If you're in the area for a few days, Den of Nargun (*see* p.20) is about a half-hour drive away.

#TWOHOURSOUT
Calembeen Park

It is perhaps Calembeen Park's restored diving towers that make it one of the most popular swimming holes for families and teens in the town of Creswick and surrounds. With three levels, the towers add a great element of adventure to one's summer escape and get our adrenalin pumping! The park also boasts two beautiful lakes and a toddlers' pool open during the summer months, as well as the chance for you to fish, cycle and take a walk around in search of the various birdlife and waterlily displays. While you're here, we recommend you explore the village of Creswick itself, which really is an up-and-coming tourist destination with gold rush-era shopfronts, the Creswick Woollen Mills and some of the best croque monsieur you'll ever find at Le Péché Gourmand (*see* p.82)

SAFETY TIP

It's important to note that swimming holes are special places and need to be respected. You should never dive or jump in without knowing the depth or what's underneath. Rivers are active waterways and rocks and logs can be swept down in a flood, continually changing submerged hazards. Sometimes the water can be extremely chilly and the shock on a hot day can be a health hazard in itself. Never swim alone.

LEFT Allans Flat Reserve
OPPOSITE Blue Pool

#ONEANDAHALFHOURSOUT

Diamond Bay

JAY DILLON

When tasked with the job of writing about the lesser-known places across Victoria, one is bound to mention a few places that the locals would prefer remained a secret. Diamond Bay is definitely one of those places and we give our heartfelt apologies to the residents of Sorrento.

Almost the perfect dimensions for an AFL oval, this protected bay lies three blocks back from the main road that runs from Sorrento to Blairgowie. The non-existent carpark means it's well worth considering parking out on Melbourne Rd or even taking the 787 bus from Sorrento or Blairgowrie on a particularly good 'beach day'.

The view from the timber deck is stunning, especially at sunset, and you might like to try the panorama setting on your phone camera in order to capture the full glory of the bay. The staircase takes you down onto the caramel sand, which in turn stretches out to meet the gentle lapping of the sparkling turquoise water. The sandstone cliffs surrounding the bay are reminiscent of the small bays along the Great Ocean Road with layered sand compositions running from pale blonde to ochre.

Due to the bay being protected by two rocky outcrops, this is one of the calmer spots on the ocean side of the Mornington Peninsula and a relatively safe place for a swim. Of course, you should check conditions and make your own assessment on the day and be prepared for icy freshness because ... Victoria!

Diamond Bay is part of the Coastal Walk that traverses the 30km of tea tree-covered cliff-tops and beaches facing Bass Strait from Cape Schanck Lighthouse to Point Nepean National Park. If time isn't on your side, then heading east along the coast from Diamond Bay will take you to St Paul's lookout and the view across a collection of small rocky outcrops known as the Bay of Islands. Taking the west trail along the cliff-tops will connect you to Coppins Track with excellent views to Sorrento as the sun sets.

Be sure to stick to the beach and designated pathways, as the area is undergoing an extensive revegetation program and contains a number of fragile middens.

WHY STOP THERE

If you do decide to do the Coastal Walk towards Cape Schanck, the truly adventurous can then join the Two Bays Walking Track in order to cross the peninsula over to Dromana. This 26km trail will take you through lush green fern gullies, the eucalypt forests of Greens Bush and climb to an elevation of almost 300m above sea level as you cross Arthurs Seat.

The temptation then is to join the 28km Bay Trail all the way back to Sorrento to complete the ultimate 100km walking tour of the Mornington Peninsula.

More sandy favourites

#THREEHOURSOUT
Fairy Cove

Wilsons Promontory is well loved and well explored by Victorians. It still holds a few secrets though, and Fairy Cove is one that doesn't require a full-day hike.

After about a 20min drive from the park entrance, park in the Darby River carpark and look for the Fairy Cove/Tongue Point signpost. This track takes you up a short climb with magnificent views back across the Darby River flood plains, through a sheoak forest and past austral grass trees. Your first peek of Fairy Cove will be from high above, and on a sunny day you'll get a view of crystal clear waters. Even in the peak of summer, we usually only come across a few people as we explore the massive granite boulders at the edges of the beach.

#THREEHOURSOUT
Childers Cove

As the Great Ocean Road heads inland around Peterborough, Childers Cove makes an excellent option to turn off and escape the caravans and tour buses. From the carpark it's a short walk down the timber staircase onto the golden sand surrounded by towering sandstone cliffs. The cantankerous Southern Ocean finds its way easily through here, so we don't recommend anything more than a knee-high wade and an exploration of the rockpools.

On a calm day it's a great place for a beach picnic and, if you time it right, you might find on the drive in that Bernard is manning the farm gate for Childers Cove Cheese Company where you can buy fresh goat's milk cheese straight out of the esky.

East of Childers Cove is Murnane Bay and Sandy Cove, which are both worth a look. Sandy Cove has some of the impressive sandstone monuments that the Great Ocean Road is famous for.

#THREEHOURSOUT
Murray River beaches

The mighty Murray that snakes its way across the top of our state is a treasure trove of riverside beaches, the best of which start downstream from the weir at Yarrawonga. The long stretch of river immediately following the weir features prime beachfront locations like Forges beach, Zinettis Beach and Bruces beach. Further downstream, the town of Cobram is an excellent base for river beaches like Thompsons Beach and Big Toms Beach.

Around 20min north of Strathmerton is Ulupna Island formed between the Murray River and Ulupna Creek. This section of Barmah National Park has some premium beach frontage and free camping, including Ulupna Beach camping ground and Carters Beach. And lastly, the section of river around Tocumwal offers some excellent beach options surrounded by huge river red gums like at Guilmartins beach and Bouchiers beach.

LEFT Murray River OPPOSITE Fairy Cove

Five great waterfalls

RICHARD CORNISH

It's the anticipation of the spectacle that we love most about waterfalls. It's that hissing roar that we hear before we see, as tonnes of water hurtle out over a rocky ledge to float seemingly slowly down through the air, only to thunder once more as the water hits the rocks below. Sometimes, often in summer, the flow is reduced to a thin veil that showers down, the warm breeze picking up the spray and covering your face and arms with a cooling mist. A lot of Victoria's waterfalls are known sacred sites to First Nations People and signs will direct you to act respectfully. Others are set up for tourists with infrastructure like concrete paths and lights at night. Some of Victoria's most impactful falls are the ones that simply give you a special feeling – where there's a beautiful path to get to them or they're just near a great place to get a hearty lunch after traipsing down a slippery track.

#ONEHOUROUT

Kings Falls
Mornington Peninsula

Crimson rosellas fly in broad arcs across the narrow gorge. Silver banksias and black wattles cloak the steep slopes. Rains over recent years have seen the normal trickle turn into a small torrent as water pours over dark boulders tumbling down into this small, tight and almost secret valley hidden in a crease of Arthurs Seat. This is Kings Falls, a small but quite dramatic waterfall that offers a rare glimpse of what this part of the Mornington Peninsula would have looked when it was home only to the Boon Wurrung/Bunurong People. They named the 330m-high peak nearby Wonga, but Edinburgh-born Lieutenant John Murray renamed it Arthurs Seat in 1802 after the volcanic outcrop in his hometown. The beauty of this waterfall is the solitude it offers so close to Melbourne/Naarm, convenient parking and easy access to a network of tracks. We recommend including a visit to the manicured **Seawinds Gardens**, the perfect place to throw out a post-hike picnic rug and enjoy the vast views across Port Phillip. Look out for the five ceramic sculptures set into a stone wall by the late William Rickett, a beautiful acknowledgement to the Boon Wurrung/Bunurong People who were the first mob to witness the arrival of Europeans in Port Phillip in 1803.

#ONEANDAHALFHOURSOUT

Loddon Falls
Daylesford

Back in the 1800s these falls, a short horse ride from Daylesford, were a popular picnic spot. On the banks of a broad pond under the shade of candlebark trees, locals and visitors would dip their toes into the cool clear waters of the Loddon River downstream of the 20m-high cascade of water gushing over hexagonal columns of 2.5-million-year-old basalt. Today access needs to be negotiated and the walk down the gorge is for the more adventurous and sure-footed walker. Look out for reptiles, swamp wallabies, local eastern grey kangaroos and the resident wedge-tailed eagles that soar on the summer thermal currents.

The **Glenlyon General Store** is only 1km away and offers outdoor casual dining, good burgers and an excellent gin list.

#THREEHOURSOUT

Agnes Falls
Toora

Out on Victoria's perennially green coast near Toora on South Gippsland's Prom Coast, the Agnes River plunges 59m over a rock ledge to form Agnes

Falls. The fall is not sheer; instead the water cascades over boulders, creating a roaring spectacle, particularly after heavy rain. The river is surrounded by a ribbon of remnant bush, where fantails dart and play, flying up to catch termites on the wing. Kookaburras, meanwhile, sit in the towering blue gums, watching for signs of prey. This is a beautiful place with a picnic area and toilets near the carpark from which the falls are only a 200m walk.

Nearby is the historic town of Toora with a pub, cafe and access to the Great Southern Rail Trail.

#THREEANDAHALFHOURSOUT
Den of Nargun
Mitchell River National Park

Mitchell River National Park contains some of Victoria's most beautiful and intriguing landscapes. At the Den of Nargun, the Mitchell River cuts a deep gorge through the hard rock, creating dramatic escarpments. Down by the confluence of Woolshed Creek and the Mitchell River, there is a clear pool of water surrounded by callistemon trees, some with massive gnarled trunks, that must be hundreds of years old. Upstream is the eerily beautiful Den of Nargun, a site sacred to Gunai/Kurnai women, where the Woolshed Creek has created a waterfall, cave and rockpool. When we visit, we ask our daughters to go ahead and ask for permission from the local ancestors. Even small inclusions of local First Nations culture into a short visit makes it more meaningful for us (non-Indigenous) visitors and respectful to the Traditional Owners. The walk is 5km return and quite steep in places, but the scenery is dramatically beautiful.

Nearby in the town of Lindenow is a good Irish pub and **The Long Paddock**, (*see* p.168), a cafe in an old bakery offering classic country meals cooked by Michelin star chefs. Great corned beef and excellent tarts.

#FOURHOURSOUT
Wannon Falls
Cavendish

The Wannon River rises in the Grampians/Gariwerd, flows through Dunkeld, north-west to Cavendish then west to the Glenelg River at Casterton. This is river red gum country. Beautiful, rich grazing farmland, with the spectacular ancient Grampians/Gariwerd mountains to the north and the dormant cones of volcanoes to the south. Just south of Cavendish the Wannon River drops a dramatic 30m over a half-moon shelf of volcanic rock into a broad pool of water. There is more flow in winter and in summer the flow can reduce to a thin sheet. The Gunditjmara People have a deep cultural connection to this magnetic site. Colonial-era artist Thomas Clark painted the falls both from a distance and inside the falls themselves in the 1860s and his paintings are prized possessions of the National Gallery of Victoria. A short drive away is **Nigretta Falls,** which are equally spectacular, whether taken in from the viewing platform or by scrambling down to the base.

Not far away is our favourite Western District pub **The Bunyip Hotel** at Cavendish (*see* p.183) where ex-MoVida chef James Campbell cooks exceptionally good food from local produce.

OPPOSITE Loddon Falls
PREVIOUS Agnes Falls

#ONEANDAHALFHOURSOUT

Blackwood Mineral Springs

DELLARAM VREELAND

There are certain spots in regional Victoria that hold special places in our hearts. Mostly because of the memories we've forged there with family and friends, but also because of the awe-inspiring surroundings that they boast. Blackwood Mineral Springs is one of those places.

Every year around Boxing Day, we make the trek out to Blackwood – an incredibly lush and picturesque village nestled in Wombat State Forest just over an hour's drive outside Melbourne CBD. Sporting our finest togs, and with our picnic gear in tow, we set up base by the banks of the glistening Lerderderg River as our little

ones frolic in the shallow, flowing waters and we bask in the sunlight amongst the dense Australian bush – kookaburras laughing and all. Whenever we've visited the springs, they've hardly been overcrowded, which has made the experience all the more enjoyable.

Once we've set up base by the creek, we venture further through the reserve and discover all the wondrous natural offerings. The creek itself opens up into a larger lagoon of sorts, where you can easily spend the day swimming and splashing. The younger ones always have a blast here. Or we cross the footbridge and head along one of the walking tracks which lead to a larger lake and lookout – it's yet another spot for swimming (races) and frivolity!

Entry to the reserve is by gold coin donation, which allows for the facilities to remain in top nick. There are undercover picnic areas with tables and toilets, and of course a chance to sample the mineral springs. And while there are barbecues at the reserve, we like to take along our own Weber and set up right by the river so we can cook, observe and play all at once.

Sometimes, we even set up base at the rustic **Blackwood Mineral Springs Caravan Park** and make a real holiday of it. The caravan park is located above the reserve's banks, and includes all the necessary amenities you need for a comfortable stay. Surrounded by Blackwood's towering eucalypts, you have the option of booking a couple of refurbished vintage caravans, or camping on a powered or unpowered site. Exuding real old-school charm, the park features bathrooms, a playground and kitchen facilities, and is just a short stroll away from the mineral springs. One year, we happened to stay on-site on Christmas Day, and received a special visit from Santa Claus aboard his fire truck, sharing joy, candy canes and merriment for all.

It's all these moments and more that make Blackwood Mineral Springs one of the sweetest spots for us to visit and one of the most soul-refreshing places in regional Victoria.

FUN FACT

The mineral springs here have travelled deep underground for several kilometres. In 1887, they were described by the government analyst as the equal of 'Appolinaris' – an expensive European natural sparkling mineral water. With a significant reduction in chloride and sulphate concentrations over the last century, the waters have even improved with age.

JOURNEY TO THE CENTRE OF ERTH

Blackwood is home to the renowned **Gardens of St Erth**, a secluded yet magnificent cottage garden that offers something different with every passing season – from carpets of daffodils in spring to stunning auburn blooms in the autumn. Boasting a dry garden, orchard, bush garden and kitchen garden, St Erth is an inspiration to both experienced and aspiring gardeners alike. The gardens also feature an on-site cafe, as well as the Diggers Garden Shop – housed within the original sandstone cottage from the garden's gold-rush days and stocking a range of edibles, perennials, shrubs and seeds.

#FIVEHOURSOUT

Lower Glenelg River (Bochara)

JAY DILLON

Suddenly it was as if we had taken front-row seats at a 12pm matinee show. For the last hour or so my canoeing partner and I had mostly focused on our own paddling techniques, ribbing each other about who was getting a free ride and pausing for the important distribution of lolly snakes. Now, we were just passive passengers of the river, flowing in silence, marvelling at dancing welcome swallows that sped and turned across our bow, retreating to small caves set in the towering limestone walls that surrounded us.

A canoe trip along the Lower Glenelg River is a magical journey through one of the most isolated parts of Victoria (with a 3km dip into South Australia) and an opportunity to be close to nature that isn't always possible in other waterways. The Glenelg River itself forms in Gariwerd/Grampians, flowing initially west to Harrow and then turning south towards Casterton. The designated canoe trail that passes through the Lower Glenelg National Park is managed by Parks Victoria and runs from the town of Dartmoor to the river mouth at Nelson.

The Gunditjmara, Wotjobaluk and Boandik Peoples all have an ongoing deep spiritual connection to the river developed over thousands of years. The river is a boundary for the three Nations and known by the name Bochara to the Gunditjmara People, Bugara to the Wotjobaluk People and Pawur to the Boandik People. It has provided not only water and food, but also served as a place of ceremony, storytelling and communal gathering. We were fascinated to learn of a recent trial involving Traditional cultural burning to reduce fuel load of the understorey whilst protecting the food source of the south-eastern red tail cockatoo in the upper canopy. It is humbling to think that many of the solutions for reversing the environmental loss and damage that started with the arrival of European settlers likely lie with the First Nations cultures that were so quickly displaced from the land.

Major Thomas Mitchell first surveyed the Glenelg River in August 1836 on his third major expedition that started when his party crossed the Murray River and continued south to what would become the site of Nelson until he ultimately discovered a whaling outpost at Portland. European settlements then started to appear from the 1870s, with the river quickly becoming recognised as an excellent location for recreational fishing by the residents of Mount Gambier in South Australia and the Western District of Victoria who often built small shacks on the banks. The majority of these river shacks were removed when the Lower Glenelg National Park was declared in 1969, although some still remain in the South Australian section and on the approach to Nelson.

There are seven canoe campsites and an additional nine drive-in riverside campsites, all with toilets, picnic tables and fireplaces. Dartmoor to Nelson is generally considered a four-day adventure, but it's quite easy to choose to do sections in three- or even two-day trips. The canoe-only campsites are placed apart in the range of 10 to 14km, which is an achievable distance to canoe – even for first-timers. For the leisurely paddler and those with young kids these distances can be shortened further by utilising the drive-in campsites as well.

Each of the canoe campsites has its own timber landing deck that provides easy access for loading and unloading your gear. Locations need to be booked in advance via the Parks Victoria website (parks.vic.gov.au) and this ensures that there is only ever one or two other groups camping at each location. Sharing stories from the day's paddle with new friends is actually one of the most enjoyable parts of the trip – and very handy if you forget an essential piece of equipment as there is a real community feel on the river.

The large storage area of a canoe allows for some bulkier items to be carried that would never be part of a hike, such as a couple of fold-up chairs and some pieces of slow-burning red gum for creating the perfect end-of-day place to gather around the campsite with a hot cup of tea, watch the kids toast (and often burn) marshmallows and enjoy the call and return of the boobook (a native owl) from somewhere in the dark.

The birdlife of the Glenelg River is extraordinary, stacked in layers like an avian tiramisu. At the very top are the ever-impressive wedge-tailed eagles, taking in their domain from some 1000 metres above the forests with barely a flap of their wings. Next layer down is filled with all manner of cockatoos with groups of 15 or so yellow-tailed black cockatoos commonly sighted. This is also the domain of the south-eastern red-tailed black cockatoo who, unfortunately, haven't been able to adapt to the changing habitat as well as their yellow-tailed friends – and are now listed as endangered. Weaving between the trees are rosellas, parrots, kookaburras and honeyeaters. The river itself is the stage for the very hard-to-find azure and sacred kingfishers and herons, and you might spot a cormorant victoriously drying its wings from a-top a riverside log. Around our campsite willie wagtails, fantails and fairy-wrens kept us constantly entertained with their bouncing and bobbing in search of a stray crumb.

As the sun goes down, the fish really start to get active. We would never recommend relying on caught fish as your food source, but if you do pack some light fishing gear and a tub of sandworms there's a good chance your instant pasta will become the side dish for a freshly caught black bream (a current fishing licence is required).

The upper section between the Moleside and Pritchards landings is a haven for koalas, some dozing comfortably in gums overhanging the river where you can paddle up for a closer look. Platypus are present for those lucky enough to catch a glimpse, wallabies and potoroos can be sighted on the banks and every campsite seems to have a naughty possum in residence.

There are canoe and kayak hire businesses in Dartmoor, Winnap and Nelson and we found them all very helpful in providing pre-planning advice. For a small additional fee they will drive you up to your launching place and offer safety advice before you set off.

We are convinced that a canoe trip along the Lower Glenelg River should become an official rite of passage for all Victorians.

SPEND A LITTLE TIME IN NELSON

It's a big drive from anywhere to get to the river, so to ensure you get an early start on the first day of canoeing it's wise to spend the first night in Nelson. Nelson is a very cute coastal town consisting of not much more than a shop and a pub.

The **Nelson Hotel** is a real classic old-school watering hole where the locals gather on a Friday night for the meat raffle and a chat. The pub grub is top-notch and we love that they still do a help-your-self salad bar.

The Kiosk is stocked with lots of camping and fishing supplies and it will likely have the items you realised on the drive down that you forgot to pack. The thought of biting down into their excellent house-made pies and sausage rolls will be the driving force for your final day of paddling.

Where we shop

Let's just agree that in holiday mode we're all more likely to feel those spending floodgates open. Just a touch. The permission to spend is more easily granted (by ourselves, of course). But then again, why wouldn't it be? We are in holiday mode, after all.

As you tour across regional Victoria on daytrips or weekends away, you are bound to come across some stellar shopping destinations that will lure you with their country charms. Many of the boutiques are owned by passionate makers and producers who have decided to make a living for themselves on the outskirts of the big smoke, pursuing their dreams in a space that you'll only come to know about by word of mouth – and from this book.

Head to the centre of Ballarat where you will find the Unicorn Hotel, not only the most gloriously named building, but also the site for Windflower (see p. 52) – a floristry and boutique retailer that is as pretty as a picture and will have you weak at the knees. Travel north-east to Yackandandah and you'll discover the unique custom hat retailer Feather & Drum (see p. 34). Venture down south and you'll be able to savour the seaside views and collective creations at Dromana Habitat (see p. 42). And head to the north and you can immerse yourself in a sea of nostalgia and quirky delights at Bendigo Antiques and Collectibles Centre (see p. 57).

Though the next few pages will divulge but a few of our favourite regional retailers, here's a hot tip: Victoria's villages are *all* filled with character and charm – and their shops are similarly so. There are vintage fashion stores (check out Warburton, Maldon and Castlemaine for some of our go-tos), stationery boutiques (Bendigo and Geelong have a couple of winners), suave jewellery designers (in Warracknabeal, for instance), and a whole collection of stellar independent bookshops (see p.49) in both coastal and country towns. So no matter where you're visiting, whether it's the tiny hamlet of Rushworth or a larger centre like Werribee, you'll be flooded with a smorgasbord of choice.

Let's go shopping.

#THREEHOURSOUT

Feather & Drum Custom Hat Co.

JAY DILLON

Until the 'before times' pre 2020, Cat Leahy had been a professional touring musician and band booker, used to being on the road and playing to audiences around the globe with the High Country town of Yackandandah as her home base.

The cessation of international travel left Cat with the mental space to explore other creative avenues and she remembered a past fascination with hat making. Rather than just fall down an internet rabbit hole of pretty Pinterest pics, Cat sought out some practical tuition via world-renowned milliner Waltraud Reiner. The virus even cut that short, and after just two days of what should have been seven days of hands-on training, Cat stayed home like everyone else in Victoria and learned how to make traditional felt hats.

The power of social media, combined with a huge network of friends in the music industry, meant this novice suddenly found herself with a months-long waitlist for her lids. When her neighbours on the main Yack drag suggested she take over their

shopfront lease, she initially scoffed – Cat had no retail experience, didn't know how to run a store and wanted to get back to gigging the minute the borders reopened. As it turns out, none of those things mattered and a middle-of-the-night vision of what the space could look like now sits proudly at number 2 High St.

Gold leaf, handpainted signwriting hollers Feather & Drum's name at passersby and, as you cross the

threshold into what's essentially Cat's workroom, there's a distinct Western (as in country) feel, with rawhide rugs on the polished pine floorboards and an enormous, three-dimensional silver star up on the wall that oversees the collection of traditional, vintage wooden hat blocks that are used to shape and create each piece.

Most of Cat's hats are bespoke and made in collaboration with the wearer; being measured, choosing your trim, colour, embellishments and having a chat about what you want your hat to tell the world about who you are, are all part of the experience. This is the epitome of slow fashion and it is worth the wait to have a wearable heirloom that's a truly unique, tangible symbol of self-expression. Rock stars, hipsters, farmers, fashionistas and everyone in between go through this process at Feather & Drum and, now that live music is back in full swing, Cat can spot her work in a crowd from a mile away.

In amongst the wooden spools of shimmering coloured threads and delicately embroidered braids, there are some off-the-rack hats that you just might be lucky enough to have a Cinderella moment with, and walk out with your new accessory bestie on the day. These ready-to-wear pieces are also one-of-a-kind and handmade by Cat, who imagines the wearer in her mind's eye as she's making them, and is always surprised and delighted when that person just happens to visit her shop in Yack. A true match, made in millinery heaven and worth a try on whenever you're in town.

YACK AROUND

We could spend an eternity wandering the leafy streets of Yackandanah. A few minutes' north of the town, a separate precinct has popped up at the site of the old Yakandandah railway station. It was one of the first railway lines in Victoria and it was where the engine was turned around to head back to Beechworth.

Blackwood Distillery is one of the main tenants, started by Myrtleford couple Lee and Bree Attwood, who started distilling, initially in their backyard, after falling in love with Tasmanian whisky. The distillery door is designed for visitors to experience the complete grain-to-bottle journey. It's a big open space where you can enjoy a tasting paddle and order in snacks from cafe **The Guard** next door.

Another favourite in the station precinct is artisan baker **Happy Baker**. It is run by late-career baker Michael Quealy, who bakes three times a week with a focus on just serving the local community (although plenty of visitors are following the scent of freshly baked sourdough). Using stone-ground flour from nearby Woodstock Flour and berries and fruit that are dropped off by locals, this is a truly locals' bakery worth seeking out.

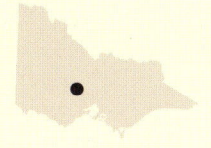

#ONEHOUROUT

Royal George Hotel

JAY DILLON

Throughout our travels since the end of the Covid lockdowns, we have heard many stories of change and adaptation from small-town business owners. For some, it was just a matter of no more office meetings, or turning to pick-up or home delivery. Then for others, like the Royal George Hotel in Kyneton, it was a fundamental change of what the business was all about, creating a whole new experience for visitors and reigniting a passion for the owners.

Long-time hospitality entrepreneurs Frank and Melissa had only taken over the Royal George Hotel kitchen for a year before the business had to close due to the increasing threat of the pandemic. Not only did they find themselves as the owners of a gastro pub with no customers, but there was the extra burden of Melissa's boutique homewares store, Kabinett, a few doors down.

After a short period of quiet despondency, Frank and Melissa decided to strip the interior back to its bare bones and move the furnishings from Kabinett into the downstairs area of the pub with the hope of at least keeping one business open and alive. And their hope paid off as now, post-lockdowns, the business is more than just alive – it thrives.

As you enter the pub, your eyes must adjust to both the low light and the bewildering sight of rooms filled with multi-period furnishings pulled from institutions, offices and workshops from across the world.

Melissa has 14 years' experience of sourcing unique furniture and homeware pieces, taking visitors on a sensory journey of their own past memories abroad. Although the pieces are sourced from across the globe, there is a definite nod to mid-century styling and within this an interesting friction between modern clean lines and the layered patina of vintage.

Up the dark carpeted stairwell the journey continues, including a range of smaller items like candles, prints and plants. In the corner is a display of six European fragrance houses like Naomi Goodsir and Memo, showcasing a variety of single-note scents through to complex botanicals designed to invoke memories of travel to places as far away as Ireland and Sicily.

Many of the fragrance houses selected also distil their own alcohol such as amaro and vermouth and it is not by chance that the neighbouring section is a wall of aromatised wines with flamboyant postwar typography.

In what could quite possibly be the largest collection in Australia, the shelves are stacked with a dazzling selection of aperitivo, bitters, vermouth and amaros, plus liqueurs and botanicals that are integral to cocktail making. Surprisingly, every single item is available to taste and the staff are more than happy to educate you on the fascinating world of aromatised wines.

You'll also notice the resplendent bar area dressed in green and gold and you'll come to the realisation that Frank and Melissa have been taking you on a sensory travel journey this whole time ... and now it's time for a drink. *Cin cin!*

When the lockdown restrictions were relaxed, the cocktail bar was created as a place for locals to gather and connect again. Whenever we are in town, we make a beeline for Botanik to escape the heat and have a surprising drink or two. We love to sit up at the bar where all the action is and it's the perfect spot to meet new people and sometimes have the chance to share a drink and a laugh with the owners. If you're in a small group, head out onto the verandah (which also functions as a plant nursery), to find a secluded table set amongst the greenery and enjoy a drink with charcuterie. Don a pith helmet if you really want to blend in with the jungle safari vibes.

The wine and beer list is well considered, but it's Frank and Melissa's knowledge of cocktails that should really be taken advantage of. Cocktails can even be ordered deconstructed, where they are served separately in different vessels allowing you to make the connection to the various layers before pouring over ice to experience the amalgamation of the different parts.

What was once a small-town pub with beer stains and parmas has become a multi-sensory department store lifted from the centre of the likes of Copenhagen or Munich. Towards the end of the lockdown period, this place was an almost spiritual experience that brought a tear to the eye of more than a few visitors.

For Melissa and Frank, being forced to reconsider what service a pub is meant to provide has given them the opportunity to create something that is a true expression of their interests and passions. It's not for everyone of course and from time to time someone will comment that they have ruined the pub. Melissa's response is to tell them to go upstairs, have a browse, talk to the staff, enjoy a cocktail then come back and tell her if they still think it's ruined. None have yet to return.

WHERE WE SHOP 41

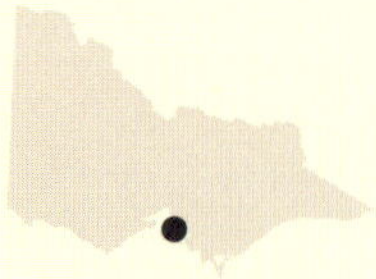

#ONEHOUROUT

Dromana Habitat

JAY DILLON

Dromana certainly isn't the first beachside location that has seen its start-ups and contemporary retailers take advantage of the relatively cheap rents available in the town's industrial estate. It's not even the first place on the Mornington Peninsula to do it but what makes the Dromana Habitat different is that, when many of the small businesses in this collection of warehouses recognised the shared values and ambitions of their neighbours, they formed a *collective*.

From a fiscal point of view this makes obvious sense – share costs and improve everyone's bottom line. The real innovation though, and what put the Habitat on our map, is that this forgotten pocket of the wrong side of the freeway has suddenly become a destination all of its own.

The turn-off to the industrial estate is opposite the cult favourite Dromana Drive-In (yes, still functioning; yes, still as fun as you remember) and trust your sat-nav as you round the grassy bend; you're definitely going in the right direction.

Remember, there have been factories and workshops down here for decades, so you have to hunt for the hidden gems within open (roller) door spaces. Part of their ethos is connection – to people, to place, to product – so they absolutely invite you to wander in, poke around, try, taste and have a chat.

If you're familiar with the 'Ninch, you'll probably recognise the signage of stalwarts **Little Rebel** and **Jetty Road**. So, start your exploration by popping in for a brew of either the caffeine or beer variety.

Red Hill Candle Co. and **Bass and Flinders Distillery** have been coaxed down from Red Hill to take advantage of a bigger space to expand their ranges and offer classes to share the skills, passion and knowledge of their crafts.

The seaside location surrounded by paddocks is justification for visitors to access fresh seafood from **Peninsula Fresh Seafood** and then pop up the road for artisan cheese from **Boatshed Cheese** and **MP Cheese Merchants**. Plus, it wouldn't be hot on the zeitgeist if there weren't indoor plants from **Verdant Dwellings** and sans-animal dairy from **The Vegan Dairy** in the line-up.

We like to pop in for a pinot at **Rhino Tiger Bear**, a self-described 'urban cellar door', who use local grapes but create and sell their cool-climate varietals away from the vineyard. The wines are also unique in that husband-and-wife duo Owen and Rhiannon insist on making only biodynamic and additive-free drops and use their big academic brains to meld science degrees with ye-olde-worlde vinification.

If an onshore is blowing, we prefer to warm our cockles with a nip from **JimmyRum Distillery**, who are determined to take the bogan out of cane spirits and bring a sense of theatre, refinement and uniqueness to the flavours they distil on-site and age in the barrels behind the bar. Like all good pirates they start pouring at 10am, so climb aboard and join the 'it's always midday somewhere' crew.

Full of Dutch courage is the only time we're ever happy to try on jeans, so after a couple of drinks the coast is clear to head to **Everwear Denim** and get measured up by Lee May for a bespoke pair. Lee literally cut his tailor chops on Savile Row in London, and now whips up pairs on his 80-year-old sewing machine, using Japanese selvedge denim to create truly unique and made-to-last garments. Sure, you have to come back to pick up your pants when they're ready, but what a perfect excuse to visit again and continue to explore the Habitat.

LOCAL TIP

An important point to note is that traditional retail hours are not followed in this part of the world. If the surf's pumping expect to find a 'closed' sign or be understanding that 'small batch' often means small teams, who might be making out the back some days, and not necessarily selling on the day you visit.

If you find yourself disappointed on arrival, fear not – we've got one last hot Dromana tip: **Miller's Bread Kitchen** is less than 2km from the Habitat and daily bakes fresh sourdough loaves, fluffy focaccias, overstuffed sandwiches, unctuous pies, golden sausage rolls and they have a cake cabinet guaranteed to make you salivate. Not a bad consolation prize if you've driven from the city.

#THREEHOURSOUT

Beechworth Conservatory

DELLARAM VREELAND

The motto at Beechworth Conservatory reads 'today is a good day to have a good day'. It's a pretty apt catch-cry for a space that evokes joy, goodness and pure delight.

The Conservatory is an all-embracing venue nestled on the outer edge of the historic township of Beechworth. It's a nursery, a cafe, an accommodation space and a hub aimed at gathering people together over a good brew and an even better chinwag.

Owned by high-school sweethearts Meg and Ollie, the Conservatory kind of just happened upon them by accident. Meg and Ollie discovered their love for plant-keeping during the pandemic while others were finding their calling baking sourdough. As the couple's love for plants grew, so did their collection, and soon they had a storefront that shared their newfound hobby with other plant aficionados. Originally meant to be used as an office set-up for their graphic design ventures, the building morphed into something much more – and we're glad that it did.

Lush plants of all forms and hues are scattered throughout the Conservatory, each with whimsically designed care-cards that can add a lot more meaning to your plant-owning experience. It's a creative point of difference between this nursery – if that's what you can call it – and others around the traps.

Coffees are enthusiastically conjured up front too, served alongside a rotating menu of Persian love cakes, custard tarts, brownies, pfeffernusse and more from the local **Happy Baker** (*see* p.37).

The accommodation continues on with the same eclectic theme. There are bold colours and whimsical artworks, abundant foliage and light-filled corridors, vintage furniture and textured bedding – all of which makes for a charming weekend away.

One of the oldest buildings in Beechworth, this quiet shanty on the road into town is fast becoming a treasured asset in the local community and beyond. It's a place to relax, connect with friends or simply savour the green gorgeousness that surrounds you.

WHILE YOU'RE HERE

For the love of all that is edible, don't come to Beechworth without an appetite! Coffee aficionados will be well-satisfied at **Tiny** on Camp Street. On the main drag is **Project 49**, a providore that is the perfect gateway to the best produce and wine of the region. Across the road is **FarmacyCo**, a herbal apothecary, where owner Naomi will guide you through the world of medicinal herbs and seeds (she makes killer fresh juices too). At the southern end of town, next to Bridge Road Brewery, is the award-winning **Eldorado Road** cellar door, which offers excellent tastings with small dishes to match. And come dinner time, Chef Sean Ford is setting the standard for French and Italian fine dining at **The Ox and Hound Bistro**.

Bookshops

DELLARAM VREELAND

Melbourne is a UNESCO City of Literature and renowned for its bookstores and literary events, and this bookish vibe spreads all across the state.

Now that Victorians can travel again, many of us have taken our reading habits with us on the road – we look for a break in activities to get stuck into a good book, especially when the sun is seeping down on us, or we're sitting outside our accommodation under the shade of a spotted gum, or making the most of a rainy day by finding a cosy nook inside.

If you are on the road and searching for a great read, there are plenty of wonderful independent bookstores in coastal and country towns throughout Victoria. Here's a list of some of our favourites.

#ONEHOUROUT
Verso Books
Healesville

Nina and the passionate team of bookworms at Verso Books in Healesville served the local community well during the Covid lockdown periods, with local home delivery or pick-up. Now this Yarra Valley beauty is once again filled to the brim with all the best new books and open for serious browsing and buying. Verso Books specialises in new-release fiction, gardening, food and wine, art and design, current affairs and an extensive range of beautiful children's picture books.

#ONEANDAHALFHOURSOUT
The Bookshop at Queenscliff
Queenscliff

Boasting all the literary goodness and seaside holiday vibes you could hope for, combined with a charm that can only be felt from a passionate family-run business, The Bookshop at Queenscliff is a real sanctuary. Owned by a local couple (she is an author), this corner-store bookshop is packed full of topical non-fiction, holiday reads, cookbooks and a curated selection of children's picture books and fiction, as well as jigsaw puzzles for those long summer afternoons.

#ONEANDAHALFHOURSOUT
Bookgrove
Ocean Grove

There's not a whole lot of things that scream holiday more than basking the day away by the seaside with a good book in hand. Nestled in the coastal hamlet of Ocean Grove, this aptly named independent bookstore is not only a rich repository of beach tales, but is full to the brim with a plethora of fiction and non-fiction reads, cookbooks and travel books. There's a sweet dedicated children's section, and if you peruse the shop's Instagram page you can keep up to date with special author events to link in with your holiday.

#ONEANDAHALFHOURSOUT
Heads and Tales Bookstore
Barwon Heads

Yet another seaside wonder, this cosy Barwon Heads bookshop is one of the newest kids on the block, having only opened its doors during the research phase of this very book! Boasting floor-to-ceiling shelves, Heads and Tales will beckon you to fossick through its colourful spines in search of your next compelling read. And with such super friendly staff, you might just stay way longer than you meant to.

OPPOSITE Verso Books

#TWOHOURSOUT
Turn the Page Bookshop
Phillip Island

One of Phillip Island's most-treasured spots, Turn the Page is renowned for its friendly customer service, product knowledge and nifty children's corner. With comfy chairs scattered throughout the store, expect to wander in and escape to a world you'd rather be in as you lose yourself in the words and surrounds.

#ONEANDAHALFHOURSOUT
Need2Read
Warragul

Located in Warragul, Need2Read is a family-owned independent bookstore with excellent customer service to help bookworms source the perfect reads for themselves and their loved ones. With floor-to-ceiling shelves and a bright, contemporary interior, this bookstore is the town's real pride and joy.

#ONEANDAHALFHOURSOUT
The Known World
Ballarat

Taken straight out of Diagon Alley, The Known World is a real book-lovers' refuge. Housed in a 19th-century Ballarat building in one of the city's most historic thoroughfares, the space is worth visiting just in itself. As soon as you enter the doors of this second-hand bookstore, you'll be transported into a world of words and wonder, regardless of whether you make a purchase or not.

#TWOHOURSOUT
Bendigo Book Mark
Bendigo

If you can't get enough of second-hand books, Bendigo Book Mark is another one to bookmark for a visit. A beautifully laid-out independent store, the shop is a vibrant space with equally vibrant and joy-inducing reads.

#ONEHOUROUT
The Book Bird
Geelong

Founded in 2015, The Book Bird is Geelong's local, independent bookshop with a twist – because you never know what you're going to discover. Stocking a large range of new release books across all genres, this store is a repository of pure delight in literary form.

#THREEHOURSOUT
The Bright Bookshop
Bright

Stocking a range of fiction, coffee-table books, children's and YA, this bookstore is your go-to in Bright after long days on the slopes or mountain biking. It's located just near the riverside park so you can buy a book and then laze on the grass.

#TWOANDAHALFHOURSOUT
Ink Bookshop
Mansfield

Located at the foothills of Victoria's Alps region in stunning Mansfield, Ink Bookshop is an intimate alcove that surpasses all expectations. If there's a book you're after during your alpine escape, chances are that Ink will have it – its floor-to-ceiling shelves brimmed with all manner of holiday reads.

#TWOHOURSPLUSOUT
The Great Ocean Troves
Torquay and Lorne

Start your pursuit of the famed Great Ocean Road with a perusal of some famed bookstores so your seaside drive can be peppered with a delightful read or few. At the Great Ocean Road's official starting point, you'll find the Surf Coast's destination bookshop **Torquay Books**. An independent and locally owned and operated biz, this store prides itself on its extensive range of books and genres — and is particularly good for fiction, kid's books, surfing and interiors titles. Venture an hour down the road, and you'll happen upon **Lorne Books**. Also independently run and with a team of knowledgeable bookworms ready to jump to your aid should you need it, this treasure chest is packed with fiction, non-fiction and a great selection of kids' books too — all the jewels you need to complete your ocean journey.

LEFT AND OPPOSITE
The Bookshop at Queenscliff

WHERE WE SHOP

#ONEANDAHALFHOURSOUT

Windflower

DELLARAM VREELAND

Stepping into Windflower, the first thing you'll notice is how easy on the eyes she is. So easy in fact, that you'll never want to leave her warm embrace. Owned by florist Kristy Tippett, this carefully curated emporium of whimsical delights combines all of Kristy's favourite handmade objects from Ballarat and across Australia as well as a selection of seasonal blooms from her own farm and surrounding growers.

Kristy says that Windflower isn't just any florist. You won't find imported or out-of-season flowers. Here you can be certain that your purchase is not only supporting a small business but also flower farmers across the state.

While Windflower has become quite the retail destination over the last two years, the journey hasn't come without its setbacks. In January 2022, Kristy's rose farm was struck by a hailstorm, destroying 13,000 of her plants just one week out from the season's first flush. This left Kristy and her family of eight in quite the financial predicament, with the mother of six unsure if she'd be able to continue her ventures for much longer – particularly following Covid.

But in the months following the storm, Kristy had masses of loved ones and strangers alike rally around her in support of her work. And with an immense amount of effort and what seemed a defiance of all odds, the wonders of Windflower and Soho Rose Farm continue to make their mark on people everywhere.

Whenever we visit the store, we find ourselves quite mesmerised by its offerings – particularly by the shapes, hues and forms of the flowers that punctuate the space, transporting us to an alternate world.

The shop is also our favourite local spot to pick up gifts, not only because of the Ballarat-made objects we can buy (Lucky & James handmade chocolate, Grounded Pleasures Hot Chocolate, Soho Rose Farm candles and oils), but also because of the quirky bits and pieces that are sourced from across Australia, including

beautiful Robert Gordon pottery, elegant Fazeek glassware, quaint Skinny Wolf ribbons, handcrafted GM jewellery, quirky Lawn Bowls homewares and a whole lot more.

While Kristy says she's not much of a shopper herself, she says the items she chooses for the store are those she loves – which just goes to show how fine her taste is.

In early 2023, Windflower made the move from an intimate CBD shopfront to one of Ballarat's most historic buildings, The Unicorn, where it has been able to expand its product offerings as well as its calendar of workshops and events, including everything from cake decorating to candle making.

It really is a retail experience unlike any other. Get ready to peruse and be awed.

FOR A SPOT OF BRUNCH

It's hard to pinpoint one exact cafe to recommend in Ballarat for brunch. The city is an ever-evolving culinary landscape and it seems a new food offering is opening up every other week. But **Johnny Alloo** is definitely one of our favourite spots for a good coffee and even better bite. Settle into this historic corner building (named after one of Ballarat's very first restaurateurs from the gold-rush days) and admire the sleek Art Deco–inspired interior as you sip, savour and relax the day away.

WINE AND DINE

Get a decent dose of Italian fare from one of Ballarat's finest chefs, Liam Downes, at the hatted restaurant **Ragazzone**. We feel spoiled every time we dine here. The chef's changing selection is made up of classic pasta dishes turned fancy and dazzling drinks that do wonders lifting our spirits. And don't get us started on dessert. All of this served up in the confines of a supe-chic inner-city eatery. Book ahead.

A PLACE TO STAY

Boutique accommodation offerings in Ballarat are plentiful. We love the two-bedroom vintage cottage **Settler & Sons**, which is just a short stroll to Lake Wendouree. **Jean-Claude Van on a Dam** is a revamped vintage caravan set among the Australian bush, just 15min out of town. And for a complete dose of luxury, seek out the recently opened **Hotel Vera** that also houses one of Victoria's most exquisite fine dining experiences: Underbar.

#TWOHOURSOUT

Bendigo Antiques and Collectibles Centre

DELLARAM VREELAND

Tucked away beside iconic Bendigo Pottery (*see* p.59) lies a treasure trove of antiques, collectibles, homewares and vintage threads that immerses lovers of the past in a sea of nostalgic delight.

Made up of more than 40 stalls, the Bendigo Antiques and Collectibles Centre is not widely known across Victoria due to its elusive location, but also because it tends to be overshadowed by the larger and more prominent Mill Markets (located in Daylesford and Geelong – for those playing at home). But those who do know of Bendigo's offerings are likely to strike gold when visiting the centre – not surprising considering the expanse of the space. For us, it wasn't until we ventured into the pottery that we discovered its neighbour – its colours, contraptions and accoutrements lured us in. And as lovers of vintage and second-hand, we are so grateful we did.

The Antiques and Collectibles Centre is a vibrant, visual stimulation where all things kitsch, mod and antique merge into one – from vintage threads to retro homewares, antique furniture to iconic records, collectible toys to dainty jewels. We were transported away by the bustling sounds of

WHERE WE SHOP

enthusiastic shoppers foraging around the stalls, inspecting homewares, sifting through records, pulling clothes off the racks and squealing in glee at the discovery of newfound treasure.

What we loved most of all, apart from sneaking off for a quick coffee and some Devonshire tea at the on-site cafe, was the process of getting hands-on with our potential purchases and taking a moment to consider their stories. Picking up the retro coffee percolators, running our fingers over the textured doilies, and smelling the musty pages of old children's storybooks. Where had they been? Who had they belonged to? What tales could they tell if they had the chance?

It's definitely worth setting aside an hour or three to properly explore the stalls. You're bound to lose yourself in the glory of yesterday, so we recommend going in with a good idea of what you're looking for. That being said, part of the fun lies in wandering through at your own pace and browsing all the bits and bobs just waiting to be discovered. We tend to gravitate towards mugs ourselves, and managed to hunt down a suave '70s mustard mug perfect for our morning coffee before heading back into the pottery and securing another mug just to round off the entire experience. Two mugs are always better than one.

WE HAVE TO MENTION THE POTTERY

Australia's oldest working pottery, **Bendigo Pottery** was established in the 1850s when Scottish migrant George Duncan Guthrie stumbled upon a local clay deposit and went on to create the business. Throughout the years, the pottery has changed hands but remains a successful tourist attraction with its iconic wares used in high-end restaurants across the country. The site is now home to the Antiques and Collectibles Centre as well as the **Artisan Village**, made up of a group of creatives working across a range of mediums including glass bead-making, sculpting, collage, winemaking, quilting and more. So it really is worth spending a day here.

INGLEWOOD, YOU REALLY SHOULD

While you're visiting Bendigo, you'd be remiss not to venture 40min north-west of the CBD to the historic township of Inglewood – a haven of collectibles and antiques. As well as being characterised by its own charming thoroughfare, this Loddon hamlet is lined by a handful of shops, bazaars and emporiums that will further fuel your desire to seek out the finest goods from eras gone by. Just make sure to check out the individual business trading hours before popping in.

WHERE TO STAY

We recommend **Bendigo Ernest Hotel** as the place to stay during your Bendigo visit. Housed in the oldest bank in Bendigo, this hotel has been meticulously renovated to introduce stunning contemporary finishings while retaining its historic grandeur. Each suite pays homage to an Australian artist – and there's even a writers' room – with special artworks lining the suite walls and immersing guests in a rich cultural experience. The hotel is also just a few metres away from the Bendigo Art Gallery and the city's best cafes – ensuring a getaway that is immersed in art, relaxation and culture!

Where they farm

When we think about producers, our minds are typically drawn to the hard-working farmers who labour by day and night to harvest the finest fruits, vegetables, grains and meat for us to enjoy. Those who do all the hard yakka, so we can simply head to the grocery store or farmers' market and fill up our wicker baskets with the freshest fare around.

With Covid-19 and the subsequent floods around the state, Victoria's farmers have quite literally been put through the wringer. That being said, with the support of travellers who care for locally grown fresh produce, many farmers have managed to keep themselves afloat amidst the storm. So, we just want to take this moment to thank our farmers for their tireless efforts. We also want to really encourage you during your travels to buy produce that is local, to hit up as many farmers' markets as you can and to support venues that support local producers.

Victoria's cohort of producers includes a number of creative individuals who have carved out businesses that showcase incredible fare on smaller scales. Take Black Barn Farm (*see* p.77), a family-run sustainable apple orchard (plus some) and nursery, or Castlemaine's indulgent Long Paddock Cheese (*see* p.67), headed by Ivan Larcher who conjures up some of the best French-style cheeses in the country. And then there's the seafood. So much seafood. We've come up with a list of places where you can find your catch of the day (*see* p.74).

We think the term, paddock to plate, tends to be overused but, really, when you venture out into Victoria's regions, you are much more likely to experience what this really means. You'll find ingredients sourced by hard-working farmers that go directly onto your plate, a celebration of real food, made with real heart. You will meet the growers, you will understand where your food has come from and you will feel a deeper sense of connection to those who labour for our very benefit. And we think this is so important.

Let's get unearthing!

#ONEHOUROUT

Gawa Wurundjeri Resource Trail

JAY DILLON

It has been both surprising and humbling to bear witness to recent revelations that prove Victoria's First Nations People utilised sophisticated methods for the supply of food, and in direct contrast to the 'hunter and gatherer' narrative we were taught in school. These methods included planting and harvesting seeds, soil management, building dams and weirs, as well as food storage, all done in a manner designed for low impact on the environment and ensuring food supply for the long-term.

A little known tribute to First Nations farming practices has been set up by the Nillumbik Reconciliation Group, off to the side of the Yarra Glen-Eltham Rd, between Kangaroo Ground and Christmas Hills. The walk is easy, and takes only 10 to 15min, including time to read the interpretive signage that explains the pre-colonial lifestyle lived by the Wurundjeri-willam, a clan that consisted of several extended family groups who spoke Woiwurrung language and moved seasonally throughout the land until the area was gazetted in 1840 as Watsons Creek Station and disrupted completely when gold was discovered in 1854.

We sometimes stop here when taking the back way to the Yarra Valley. It's a peaceful place to rest amongst stringybark, manna gum and the bursting yellow of wattle (myuan) signalling the theoretical end to winter. Watsons Creek always seems to be in a completely different state of flow each time we visit. Echidnas waddle indifferent to our presence and wallabies pop their heads up above the grass in the distance. The signage does a fantastic job explaining how the land provided medicine, food, tools and clothing, and touches on some of the Dreaming stories too.

For example, the Wurundjeri name for the Victorian Christmas bush (*Prostanthera lasianthos*) is 'coranderrk', which was vigorously rolled between the palms to ignite dry grass and create fire. The tough branches of tea tree (burgan) were straightened out and heated over fire to create spears. We even learn how young men were sent

down the burrows of wombats (warendji) in order to signal to the men above where to lodge their spears.

The Wurundjeri People had an intimate knowledge of Watsons Creek (the Woiwurrung name was never recorded) and would take advantage of its ebbs and flows throughout the seasons. Yabbies and blackfish were plentiful and in late winter, the eels' bellies would be fat from the wattle flowers. The men would catch ducks by stringing a net across the creek and making loud noises to send them flying into the trap.

Although a short walk, the Gawa Wurundjeri Resource Trail is worth taking a little longer to linger at and make the most of the quiet time away from the rush-rush.

HABITAT CORRIDOR

Gawa Reserve is one of seven bushland reserves that make up the **Panton Hill Bushland Reserve System**. The reserves connect together to form a 140-acre corridor for native wildlife and vegetation as well as protecting some important historic sites such as the Queenstown cemetery. The reserves all feature fantastic walking and mountain-biking trails and are named after the Wurundjeri name for different species found in the area, including yanggai (yellow-tailed black cockatoo), yirrip (ironbark) and wimbi (swamp wallaby).

Each of the reserves offers something new and deserves its own day out. Nearby lunch options include **Smiths Gully Cafe**, who make a fantastic burger, and you will find excellent pizza and a glass of locally made wine at **Nillumbik Estate**.

#ONEANDAHALFHOURSOUT

Long Paddock Cheese

RICHARD CORNISH

Ivan Larcher is known globally as the cheese whisperer. He and his team make some of the best French-style cheeses in the country using local organic milk. A few years back, Ivan was living in France on his farm near Limoges, milking a few cows and crafting small batches of handmade cheese. He'd fly around the world helping small cheesemakers fix problems with their own cheeses. Then he met some cheesemakers in Central Victoria and fell in love with the burgeoning cheese scene. Backed by local business people, he brought his family to Australia and set up an artisan cheese factory and 'cheese university' in old industrial buildings in Castlemaine's The Mill precinct. In spring 2020, Long Paddock Cheese and The Cheese School opened for business.

Ivan can often be seen through the windows of the atelier working with small groups, using small-scale copper pots and pans to demonstrate to students how cheese is made in the traditional French manner.

We are big fans of French cheese and always make a beeline – esky in hand – to Long Paddock Cheese's little shop at The Mill. The range of artisan dairy is very tempting. There is single-origin non-homogenised milk – superb for frothing for coffee (or drinking straight from the bottle when no one is watching). Long Paddock yoghurt is supple and silky, screaming out to be partnered with fat ripe berries or a lightly spiced apple compote. But it is the cheese we drive here for.

The cheeses are cut and served at room temperature for tasting. Try the rippled-rinded Silver Wattle, which has a fudgy to creamy texture, depending on how ripe it is. When young, it is clean and tangy; when older it is moody and funky. We are particularly enamoured with Driftwood, a washed-rind cheese in the style of Vacherin, wrapped in spruce bark.

As the cheeses age, they develop complex aromas that layer buttery, forest floor, grass, and hay with much darker and more sophisticated aromas. Both Silver Wattle and Driftwood are perfect for slathering on fresh sourdough purchased from **Sprout Bakery** next door. Long Paddock's Tomme-style Banksia sits somewhere between a raclette and gouda, and is great for cooking, but with its notes of earth and roasted nuts, it is also an ideal companion for charcuterie.

Luckily, there is a smallgoods at The Mill too. **Oakwood Smallgoods** is owned by a German fleischermeister (master butcher) who makes exceptional pâté, hams, and bacon. Add to this a couple of crusty baguettes – made with fresh, locally milled flour and ordered from the window of the previously mentioned Sprout Bakery – and something sweet from the French chocolate house **Cabosse & Feve** next door, and you have the makings for an impressive Castlemaine picnic. We love to picnic at the Botanic Gardens across the road or, in summer, the very deep, cool and clear Castlemaine Swimming Pool on Lake Augusta Lane.

MORE FOR YOUR PICNIC

Good French cheese needs good cider. The soft cheeses from Long Paddock match well with the real cider made by the Henry family at **Henry of Harcourt**, a 10min drive from The Mill. With the summit of Mount Alexander looming dramatically on the horizon, the Henry family has planted rows and rows of old-fashioned cider apple trees with names like Kingston Black, De Bouteville and Michelin. From them, they make dry ciders more suited to enjoying with food than slugging on at the pub. Try them at the rustic cellar door, past the ornamental dam guarded by a flock of friendly ducks.

In the heart of Castlemaine is a dark and overladen wine store set in a gold rush-era building: **Castlemaine Central Wine Store**. This is the lair of wine expert Stephen Cross who learned his trade by drinking great wine. But he got sick and tired of going to bottle shops selling the same brands by the same big companies. Today he stocks only Victorian wine from small family wineries and carries 150 different lines. He specialises in local central Victorian wines and beers and personally introduced us to one of his favourites, Hanging Rock Pinot Noir, and the huge yet balanced 2018 shiraz from Mia Valley Estate near Redesdale. We can never leave seeing Steve without at least half a case of different yet delicious local wines we have never tasted before. Visiting Steve is more wine adventure than a shopping spree.

#ONEANDAHALFHOURSOUT

Flinders Mussels

RICHARD CORNISH

Harry is a Flinders icon. With his tanned face and mop of blond hair, he was a menace in the surf when he was a kid and, decades later, he is still making waves on Western Port with his mussels. Many chefs agree they are the best in the state. When we head down to Flinders, we always carry an esky to pick up a few kilos of these fat, plump, briny molluscs from Harry who sells them off his boat moored to historic Flinders pier.

Harry grows his mussels on long ropes suspended just a few metres down in the cool, clean waters of Western Port. The spat, or baby mussels, are raised in a hatchery and naturally attach to the ropes. Over a year or so the mussels filter feed in the water and grow to a mussel that will fill the palm of your hand. During the year, Harry and his crew clean the mussels and eventually bring them on board, remove them from the ropes, place them in a bin, and scoop them into a bag for customers.

There are so many good stories to tell about these mussels. They are native to the bay and have been eaten by the Boon Wurrung/Bunurong People of the area for thousands of years. The mussels filter the water, around one litre an hour, making it clean and clear. Mussels sequester carbon dioxide in their shells for thousands of years. They are also so bloody delicious, fat and juicy.

To visit Harry's boat is to take in the culture of life on the pier. There are the fishers keen to catch themselves some calamari, while on summer days the local kids will combat the 'townies' as they do 'battle of the bomb', hurling themselves off the decks of the pier into the deep water that shelters sea dragons (*see* p.154).

During summer, we also head across to Harry's food van in the carpark opposite the pier. **La Conchilia** serves up freshly cooked mussels that you can take down to the beach, where you can sit on the sand and watch the seabirds follow schools of fish as they make their way around the sheltered cove and out past the rugged rocks of West Head.

EATING IN

One of the best places to try Harry's mussels in a sit-down environment is the **Village Café and Wine Bar**, a vibrant cafe in a century-old weatherboard building in the heart of historic Flinders. Look for the picket fence and the palm tree out the front and enjoy the vibe of egalitarian luxury. You can come for coffee and brunch, the beer garden on Friday nights, or settle in for some serious eye fillet or duck confit with a bottle of Clos de Vougeot Grand Cru burgundy. With a wood-fire in winter and a sunny courtyard in summer, this local institution epitomises the Flinders lifestyle.

More ocean bounty

#TWOHOURSOUT
Sea Bounty Mussels
Portarlington

Lance Wiffen used to be a scallop fisherman but now he grows mussels down the southern end of Port Phillip at Portarlington. His native blue mussels are available year-round and are excellent in taste, texture and value. They are harvested daily and you can buy them from the little caravan at the base of the pier called **Mr Mussels** or at **Jenkins & Sons Fresh Fish** on the edge of town. Head to **Portarlington Grand Hotel** for a good feed – a big bowl of freshly cooked mussels cooked in a green Thai curry, or our favourite, Moules Provençal, the classic southern French recipe of tomatoes, white wine and garlic with sourdough bread. Look out for **Portarlington Mussel Tours** run by Lance Wiffen too on his beautifully restored wooden boat *Valerie*.

#THREEHOURSOUT
Apollo Bay Fishermen's Co-op
Apollo Bay

For 70 years, this old shed in the town of Apollo Bay has looked out over the fishing fleet as the boats sail out and return safely to the sheltered harbour below. It is still where local fish and lobsters are processed but for us it's the best fish and chips on the coast. You can also order fresh lobster and salad, grab a seat and enjoy the priceless view. Fresh fish sales are now in town at **Fresh Fish on Pascoe**. Local restaurant **Graze** also buys fish fresh from the fishers here.

#FOURANDAHALFHOURSOUT
LEFCOL
Lakes Entrance

The fishing fleet at Lakes Entrance makes its harbour in the heart of this East Gippsland village. As kids, we'd get ice-cream and clamour around the docks looking at the fish being carted ashore. Not much has changed. The boats fish Bass Strait and a few sections of coastal waters. The fish are processed at the fishermen's co-op, or LEFCOL, a few kilometres away on Bullock Island. Look out for great value species such as duck fish, sand whiting, school prawns and gurnard. The chefs at waterfront restaurant **Sodafish** buy fish fresh from the fishing boats and it's one of the best seafood restaurants, in our opinion, in the state.

#TWOHOURSOUT
San Remo Fisherman's Co-op
San Remo

When the kids were little we took them to see the pelicans being fed on the foreshore in front of the Co-op, as it is known locally. These great birds can gulp down vast flathead frames in seconds. This ritual has been going on since 1985 and happens at midday on the dot. The Co-op sells fresh local seafood such as lobsters, scallops, gummy shark and duckfish, as well as seafood from further afield. The fish and chips here are very, very good and they fry perhaps the best gummy shark in the state.

#FOURANDAHALFHOURSOUT
Arrow Fisheries
Portland

The continental shelf lies just 20km from Portland in the state's west, which means the boats in the fishery there often haul in deep-water species as well as squid, gummy shark and delicious but lesser-loved fish like Australian salmon. There is even a commercial pippi fishery at Portland. The local fish processor **Arrow Fisheries** has a retail fish store where we buy our seafood when we're in this region for a holiday. When staying in town, we visit **Pete Deegan's** fish shop. Here, you'll find rosy pink flathead fillets, gleaming baby snapper, boxes of perfect cuttlefish no bigger than your thumb, plump skate wings and fish you rarely see in the market such as hake. Deegan opens every day of the year, fries fish and chips only during the week, and on Fridays makes sushi using a recipe taught to him by a Japanese mate.

#TWOHOURSOUT
Buxton Trout and Salmon Farm
Buxton

The idea of visiting Buxton Trout and Salmon Farm is to catch your own fish. Drop a baited hook into a pond fed by the cold clean waters of the Acheron River and soon you'll have a decent-sized fish on the end of the line. Owner Mitch MacRae will clean it for you at no extra charge. While you're here check out the smoked salmon and the very luscious salmon caviar.

TOP San Remo Fisherman's Co-op
BOTTOM LEFT Apollo Bay Fishermen's Co-op
BOTTOM RIGHT Buxton Trout and Salmon Farm

WHERE THEY FARM   75

#THREEHOURSOUT

Black Barn Farm

DELLARAM VREELAND

If there's one thing the pandemic taught us, it's how vital sustainable living is: slowing down, savouring the special moments with loved ones and embracing a lifestyle focused on community, wellness and eco-friendly practices.

Perched atop Pallanganmiddang Country in the north-east gold-rush town of Stanley, Black Barn Farm is dedicated to promoting a slower, simpler and steadier existence. A biodiverse small-scale orchard, nursery and learning hub, the farm is owned by the Showers family, who have created an intentionally slow business that's regenerative in its practices and has become integral to the healthy functioning of the surrounding community.

We find ourselves in awe at the sheer beauty of the farmscape – ever-verdant and flourishing and punctuated by a country cottage, black barn and rows of makeshift stick fencing that further add to its charm. The sun-kissed orchard is just short of 750m above sea level, with the cool climate making it perfect for fruit growing. It is home to a multitude of apple varieties, pears, berries, nuts, stone fruit, quince, olives, pomegranates, figs, herbs, flowers and veggies just to name a few.

The farm's co-owner Jade Miles tells us that their practices are beyond organic: they're ecological, so there are no synthetic sprays used on-site and all the weeding is done by hand. This lends itself to a wilder landscape, a 'chaotic mess' as she calls it, but we think it just enriches the overall character of the space.

The Black Barn U-Pick program means you can forage for your own picnic or take-home goodies. Running from January until June, there are up to 100 varieties of apples and a plethora of other fruits and vegetables. Pack your own bags or baskets, or even a cooler bag or esky if you have a long drive home. And if you happen to be picking on the weekend, make sure to check out their twin sons' doughnut stand and order up the finest sugar-laden, deep-fried apple cider doughnuts in Australia (perhaps the only apple cider doughnuts in Australia, actually). Pure delight!

The fruit tree and perennial plant nursery is open during harvest season (between December and June) and the farm holds regular feasts, workshops, schools programs and events ranging from fruit grafting to plant propagation to wicking bed making. It's all part of the family's aim to connect us back to the food we eat and build a localised fair food system for the rest of society to model upon.

While you're visiting the farm, make sure to pick up Jade's book *Futuresteading*. Her book and podcast of the same name further emphasise the need to create a culture that cultivates today in order to value tomorrow. Talking with Jade really rounded off the entire experience for us – inspiring us to slow down and reconnect with our environment in search of this slow, simple and steadier existence we all so desperately seek.

MORE FARM VISITS

There are so many incredible farm experiences across Victoria that they really do deserve a book of their own! Some like **Murrnong Farm** just outside Violet Town and **Village Dreaming** near Daylesford actively invite visitors to come and learn about sustainable farming practices through tours and workshops on permaculture and traditional skills. **Rosehaven Farms** in the Wartook Valley let you get close and personal with alpacas, lambs and miniature donkeys. All while learning a few things about animal husbandry along the way.

More often though, the life of a farmer is too chaotic for such personal interaction. Many will stock a farm gate outside the property like Emma and Mikey from **Goshen Country** where you can grab some excellent market garden produce on the road between Wonthaggi and Cape Paterson. Or drop into **Jonai Farms and Meatsmiths** near Daylesford to pick up some incredible ethically raised pork products, all butchered, cooked and cured on the farm by Tammi and Stuart.

Bakeries

DELLARAM VREELAND

It's our very strong belief here at OHO that every regional road trip should start with a coffee and pastry at a local bakery. While most of Victoria's historic hamlets and country towns have their own pub and church, many of them also feature a homegrown bakery (a disproportionate number of which hold claim to the Australia's greatest pie or vanilla slice!)

It's tough to narrow down the list of our favourite bakeries in this diverse state of ours. Some of the grandest boulangeries are based in regional Victoria and are headed by talented pastry chefs or passionate bakers who have chosen to exchange the hustle and bustle of metro living for the slow country lifestyle.

We think it's a grand idea to plan your next road trip around one of the following bakeries. At least then you're assured of some deliciousness along the way. Stop off for a soft finger bun or classic chocolate eclair, or stock up on bread, cheese-and-bacon scrolls before heading off on your annual camping congregation, or simply pop in to a cafe-bakery for a decent cup of joe to fuel you for the journey ahead.

TOP Johnny Baker
OPPOSITE Maldon Bakery

#ONEANDAHALFHOURSOUT
Le Péché Gourmand
Creswick

With its name loosely translating to 'sin of gluttony' in French, this boulangerie unapologetically beckons us to indulge and we're happy to oblige. Headed by pastry chef Paul Williams and his French partner Marie, the bakery is located in the goldfields village of Creswick with the duo bringing decades of boulangerie-patisserie experience to the fore. Having originally opened in an intimate space on Creswick's main thoroughfare, it relocated a few doors down to a larger eatery a few years ago and is always bustling with locals and tourists alike. We lust for their cheesy croque monsieurs – the perfect complement to your road trip coffee.

#TWOHOURSOUT
Maldon Bakery
Maldon

Step into this characterful space in the National Trust-listed town of Maldon and you'll feel as though you've been transported to a bygone era. Owner Rebecca Barnett has restored the bakery to its former glory, reopening the old bakery quarters to the public, and stands ready to have a chat about all things baking, history and bread. With Australia's Father of Sourdough – John Downes – at its helm, the bakery also makes use of the original 19th-century scotch oven to forge wood-fired sourdough with John's magical 50-year-old leaven. Stock up on sourdough fresh out of the oven as well as gourmet pies comprising local chunky beef, cakes, tarts, cheesecakes and a selection of locally made pantry goods. There's a beautiful little garden to the side of the bakery shopfront where you can tear into your pastry bounty with abandon.

#TWOANDAHALFHOURSOUT
Tinto
Shepparton

A highly regarded micro-bakery that's as pretty as a picture, Tinto serves the local Shepparton community naturally leavened sourdough bread and yeasted pastries, and sources the finest quality and organic local ingredients. Flaky croissants, sugar-laden pastries, fruit-topped danishes, turkish bread, bagels and oh-so-much more – this place is a light-filled feast for all the senses. Pair an iced latte with a cream cheese and mushroom bagel, or indulge in a vanilla cream doughnut before pocketing a dense chocolate brownie for the road.

#TWOANDAHALFHOURSOUT
Johnny Baker
Castlemaine

Featuring two bakeries in Castlemaine – one uptown and the other downtown – Johnny Baker gets our mouths watering just thinking about its decadent offerings. Always alive with locals and out-of-towners, the patisserie is headed by pastry chef John Stekerhofs, previous co-owner and chef at Melbourne's The French Lettuce. As good a place to grab your daily brew as it is to satisfy your sweet tooth (or savoury tooth for that matter), we love treating ourselves to the dense salted caramel chocolate tarts or even a delicious scoop or two of gelato. Pull up a crate, and settle in for a special experience. Worth the drive from here, there and everywhere.

#ONEANDAHALFHOURSOUT
Ket Baker
Wallington

Headed by Belgian-born, French-trained baker Miek Paulus, this Wallington-based bakery on the Bellarine Peninsula features a stellar line-up of 100 per cent sourdough pastries, croissants, danishes, breads and all the fancy flavour profiles one can come to expect from a European boulangerie. With each product taking days to perfect before it hits the shelves, it's no wonder Ket Baker is one of the most coveted patisseries on the Bellarine and beyond. There's usually a queue of cars to get in and people lining up outside the shop, and it often sells out, so get in early.

OPPOSITE TOP LEFT Le Péché Gourmand
OPPOSITE TOP RIGHT Johnny Baker
OPPOSITE BOTTOM Maldon Bakery

WHERE THEY FARM

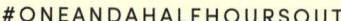

#ONEANDAHALFHOURSOUT

Inglenook Dairy

DELLARAM VREELAND

An historic dairy farm in humble Dunnstown, nestled between two of the Ballarat region's most imposing mountains (Mount Warrenheip and Mount Buninyong), Inglenook Dairy (meaning cosy corner) has fast earned a name for itself as one of the most respected and ethical farms across the industry.

Having never visited a dairy farm before, we found the interactive Inglenook tour to be quite the eye-opening experience. When you head out to the farm, you'll discover its workings for yourself and learn all about its evolution. Trust us when we say these guys have come a really long way from their humble beginnings! We particularly enjoyed the activities, such as churning cream into butter, learning all about the milk production process, and milking the cows – all amidst the stunning and serene farmscape surrounds.

The farm's journey started when co-owner Rachael Peterken's grandparents' house burned down in the early 1900s, and her grandmother's brother gifted her a bull and six cows – driving them on foot to Dunnstown to assist with the family's recovery. Thinking about how far the family farm has come – from that one small herd to now producing 25,000+ litres a week – is rather inspirational for a family-owned and -operated business.

The dairy was established in 2011 – Rachael and her husband Troy invested in their own processing plant and started manufacturing products themselves. In their mind, this was the risk they needed to take to create a top-quality product and a more sustainable future for their farm. Troy managed the entire project – leading the design of the factory along with the help of Rachael and other family members, including Rachael's parents, Basil and Sheila Britt, who were

massive advocates in the Ballarat dairy industry (and the previous owners of the farm). After two years, holding down a second job, and raising three small children, Rachael and Troy reached the point where their passion project finally came to fruition. The plant was up and running, and the Inglenook brand started making waves across the state.

A decade on, the Inglenook Dairy has a firm reputation as one of the finest producers of dairy products across Victoria – supplying cafes, supermarkets and households thanks to its smooth, delicious milk, cream, butter and yoghurt products. What's the secret? According to Troy it's nothing. Nothing but 100 per cent pure milk. No additives. Nothing watered down. It's milk the way it should be.

#ONEANDAHALFHOURSOUT

Daylesford Longhouse

DELLARAM VREELAND

A house to visit. A farmstay. A place for experimentation, conversation and the sharing of knowledge. Daylesford Longhouse has all these things going for it.

The first Victorian property to win Australian House of the Year (that should be enough to get you booking your weekend escape), this architectural dream is the project of homeowners' Trace Streeter and Ronnen Goren. The duo wanted to bring to life a vision that combined Ronnen's passion for hospitality, food and cooking and Trace's love for animal husbandry, gardening and sustainability.

The 100m-long house looks out over the vast bushlands of Daylesford and Hepburn Springs as well as the iconic Mount Franklin (Lalgambook). It comprises living quarters, a cooking school and a working farm building. Visitors can enjoy a whole array of masterclasses, lunch and learning sessions, farm tours and farmstay

experiences. Or they can simply savour the eye candy that abounds – panoramic views, a rose-coloured brick-clad bathroom of one's dreams, staircases, baby blue walls and wooden panels and scattered foliage. It's all just a feast for the senses!

The Longhouse is basically one long, lush, light-filled sunroom. You meander your way through each dedicated space in the shed, immersed in greenery, feeling as though you're perpetually wrapped in Mother Nature's warm embrace. Trace and Ronnen have seamlessly woven the outdoors in.

The living quarters are located at the far end of the home and feature bedrooms, a kitchen and dining space and can accommodate up to four guests. There are a cosy wood-fire, luxe body products, Netflix and all that jazz, and a six-foot clawfoot bathtub. You can while your days away in the lounge area, the sauna and the outdoor bathroom, and treat yourself to a bird's-eye view of the house from the viewing platform.

If you book a tour, you'll be able to venture around the farm and Longhouse, and learn about farming principles and the sustainability features of the property – from water-harvesting through to composting. You'll also meet the farm's cute critters – the dairy cows, goats and pigs – and then end your day with a sumptuous Longhouse-made treat and some refreshments.

If you're after an all-round regional experience that combines relaxation with education, slowness with fresh country air, sustainability with practicality, this is the place you need to put on top of your list. We don't like using the word unique often, but that it is.

LET ME ENTERTAIN YOU

The charming and ever-so-elegant **Palais** is a heritage-listed cultural icon in nearby Hepburn Springs and one which you must visit during your weekend sojourn. Dubbed the heirloom jewel in the crown of Victoria's spa country, this opulent yet intimate dining and entertainment venue hosts a myriad of events throughout the year – from jazz to comedy, burlesque through to classical, and everything in between, sideways and beyond. It really is a delicious melting pot of culture, food, music and old dance-hall glory.

#ONEHOUROUT

Edible Forest

JAY DILLON

Just like seeking out a cafe that roasts their own beans (I'm looking at you, Silva Coffee, *see* p.212), you know there's something special going on when a restaurant is running its own kitchen garden. Sourcing locally is one thing, but it's great to hear of chefs who have their hands actually in the soil. A really quite special example of this is the Edible Forest that is part of the Yarra Valley Estate property in Dixons Creek.

'There's actually not that much to do', says our guide, head horticulturist Jaimie Sweetman who is trying to convince me that the 0.4ha of loosely cultivated forest on a sloping hillside is actually low maintenance. As I picture the chaotic weed patch crying for help in my own backyard, she goes on to tell me that because of how the forest garden was designed, it pretty much looks after itself.

When construction began in 2016, Hugelkultur raised garden beds were built with organic materials like branches, leaves, grass clippings and cardboard around indentations designed to trap moisture. We walk past a tall lime Robinia, which we are told provides shade but also converts nitrogen in the soil into a usable form. There are several types of nitrogen-converting trees staked in key positions around the garden. Most of the work in summer is in harvesting the produce and only on the hottest of hot days does the garden require watering.

Everything has to have a reason for being here. Each planting contributes in some way, be it to attract bees or birds, to bring shade or soil health. The kitchen chef also benefits, with a kaleidoscopic collection of oddball fruits, roots, stems and for him to choose from for events and functions throughout the year. Linden leaves, gotu kola and water celery make the base for a salad. Rose hips are turned into syrup and the flowers from the Robinia tree are steeped to flavour a Turkish delight. Cordials, teas and preserves can be purchased from the Harvest Hub near the garden entrance.

As we follow the gravel trail to the bottom of the block, the temperature becomes noticeably cooler and we observe a shift from warmer climate plantings of the Mediterranean and South Africa to cool-climate plants of North America and northern Europe. Here a section is thrown over to berries from around the world. From November kids can forage through the thicket and fill their gobs with mulberries, juneberries, cape gooseberries and something called the aronia berry, which is so astringent it literally removes all semblance of moisture from our mouths.

It's not just a summer garden either. As a foraging garden, it's designed in a way that means produce can be gathered throughout the year. Come here in winter and you will find strawberry guava, medlar and midyim berries ready for picking. The large tubers of the cinnamon yam can be harvested throughout the year and then summer mini yams dangle from the actual vine, giving it the name 'air potato'.

The forest garden is a unique opportunity to see for yourself how food can be grown in a less complicated and self-sustaining way. In addition to small group tours, permaculture tours are available for those who want to dig a little deeper (excuse the pun). Those interested in learning how to utilise the garden's bounty can sign up for fermentation and preserving workshops throughout the year.

STOP FOR A DROP

There's always word of some young winemaker in the Yarra Valley doing crazy things with grape juice, and just 10min back towards Yarra Glen you will find the cellar door for **Fin Wines**. The three founders (JonJo McEvoy, Oliver Johns and Angus Hean) use wild fermentation and not much else to create exciting wines, ciders and a piquette – a low-alcohol drink made by fermenting leftover skins.

The cellar door is an open space with big timber beams, and you'll find the team out chatting with visitors rather than sitting behind a counter. The majority of tables are outside with views across their own 4ha of vines and that of neighbouring vineyards. There's a small snack menu to match your choice of wine that includes white anchovies, pâté and a mix of three cheeses.

Where
we
art

96 UNDISCOVERED VICTORIA

Arts and culture. The two terms simply roll off the tongue. In Victoria, the arts and cultural landscape can be likened to an intricately woven rug that has stood the test of time and is yet to stand for much more.

The rich cultural fabric is composed first and foremost by the original artisans, the First Nations People who have been recording culture and making artworks for tens of thousands of years. A visit to the Shepparton Art Museum (SAM) and its accompanying Kaiela Arts gallery (*see* p.117) will give but a glimpse of the phenomenon that is First Nations art.

As we continue to work through Victoria's cultural fabric, we think about the gold rush and the influence that wealth had on towns across the state from the 19th century onwards. This wealth contributed to the establishment of a number of cultural institutions unique to Victoria, with many of the museums and galleries still standing. We are speaking of the likes of the Art Gallery of Ballarat, the Bendigo Art Gallery and the Geelong Gallery. Today, they house significant works from artists all over Australia and the world. More modern establishments add to the diversity of our arts and cultural world too, such as Shepparton Art Museum, or SAM (*see* p.117), and the Benalla Art Gallery (*see* p.7), housed in an iconic modernist building in the town's stunning botanical gardens.

Today, there is an ever-growing number of artisans across Victoria who draw inspiration from Traditional Owners and from the breadth of the state's natural wonders and the unique heritage offerings to create inspiring contemporary works. Take the example of Emma Jimson and her naturally infused ceramics venture Pom-me-granite (*see* p.98), the Mount Monument Winery Sculpture Park (*see* p.102) with its organic and environmentally focused pieces, Chojo Feature Trees Gallery and Nursery (*see* p.106) with its fascinating collection of bonsai, or Geelong's Boom Gallery (*see* p.109), which showcases some of the region's finest contemporary artists.

There is much to unearth in Victoria's arts and culture scene, and even more to learn.

Let's get weaving!

#ONEANDAHALFHOURSOUT

Pom-me-granite

DELLARAM VREELAND

A couple of our favourite things. The stunning hues of auburn, crimson and yellow that can be admired in regional Victoria's lushest areas during the autumn months. And pottery.

So you can just imagine our sense of elation when both of these treasures combine at a visit to a ceramics studio nestled in one of Victoria's most iconic natural regions in the middle of the autumn season. Oh how we lust!

Charming Pom-me-granite is a ceramics studio located in picturesque Pastoria East on Taungurung Land, just a 20min drive north-east of the quaint village of Kyneton. Owned by ceramicist Emma Jimson and her carpenter husband Jim, the studio proudly sits on a farm shared with Emma's parents at the foothills of the Cobaws in the Macedon Ranges.

Emma is known for creating delicate yet functional works that are not only pleasing to the eye but also help feed our body. Her specialty is the forging of handcrafted fermenting vessels – we're talking kombucha on-tap crocks, fermenting weights, kimchi crocks, cheese forms, pickle pots, kefir strainers, miso crocks and more.

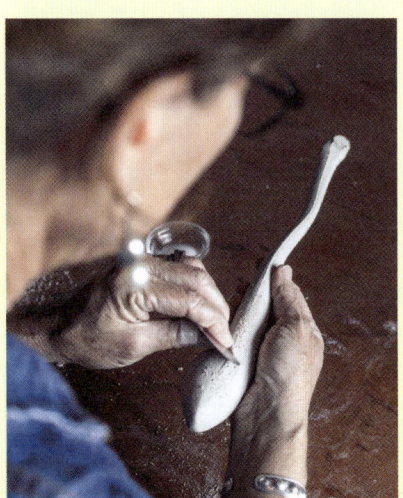

In 2023, Emma and Jim upgraded their studio space, expanding the workshop to allow for more pottery enthusiasts to experience the wonder of Pom-me-granite for themselves. A long, light-filled tin shed is divided into separate creative spaces and features an area where Emma works with her clay and hosts workshops for beginners and for other potters who want to introduce advanced slip casting into their practice. There are also spaces for mould-making, a kitchenette,

a retail space showcasing everything from porcelain tableware to fermenting vessels, wooden boards and lavender products from the paddock, as well as a generous woodworking area for Jim.

Emma and Jim draw much of the inspiration for their work from their home's surroundings. When we visited, it was easy to see how the abounding granite formations, on-site lavender plantation, native trees and majestic mountains would do wonders to influence the natural composition and design of the couple's art. The landscape certainly sets the scene for an immersive, serene and ultra-therapeutic experience when you visit.

To be fair, this part of regional Victoria is divine any time of year – its expansive forests and iconic landscapes draw us in over and over again. (We also loved visiting the studio in the late spring to summer when the lavender was in full bloom, right before it got harvested and distilled into premium lavender oil.) So regardless of what season it is, just make sure you make a point of venturing out here. Whether you consider yourself a beginner with clay or a pro potter, Emma will up your confidence with her gentle guidance and inspiring manner, and you'll leave Pastoria East with a beautiful object you're sure to cherish forever.

NEARBY TIPPLE

About a decade ago, couple Renata and Ollie purchased a small vineyard and home not long after Ollie had completed his viticulture qualifications. They renamed the property **Lyons Will Estate** after their prospective mentors. Here they have raised a family and produced some stunning wines from the cool climate of the Macedon Ranges. The cellar door recently had a makeover with lots of black steel and stone, and hosts sit-down tastings with views across the vineyard. It's worth booking ahead, as despite the feeling of being out in the middle of nowhere, those in the know come regularly to enjoy cool-climate pinot noir, chardonnay and some seriously good charcuterie.

#ONEANDAHALFHOURSOUT

Mount Monument

JAY DILLON

Whenever we have visitors from interstate, we like to include an outdoor sculpture park as part of the itinerary (weather permitting, this is Victoria after all!). The Mornington Peninsula has Pt. Leo Estate and McClelland Sculpture Park; Hanging Rock Winery has an annual sculpture exhibition; there's the Yindyamarra Sculpture Walk that tells First Nations stories amongst the Wonga wetlands; and more recently a small sculpture park popped up at Mount Monument – a cool-climate winery in the Macedon Ranges.

It's a transcending experience to walk amongst structures and shapes of various materials in a landscape where they really shouldn't belong. And quite often there's a fantastic spot to lay out a picnic and let the kids roam free, too.

We first started hearing whispers of earth moving and oddly shaped deliveries arriving at a property near Romsey in early 2022. It was with a tinge of disappointment we found it wasn't the construction of a secret military facility for paranormal experiments, but rather a personal project of highly awarded architect Nonda Katsalidis (MONA, Eureka Tower, Levantine Hill Estate, to name a few) and partner Jane Collins.

The couple purchased the 45ha property in 2005, and had been slowly working to regenerate the land by focusing on water management and increasing animal life and birdlife. Through hard work and lots of patience, the large dam at the base of the property is slowly transforming from its purely agricultural function to a biodiverse wetland. The buildings include water tanks and composting worm farms as part of their design and are built using fire-resistant materials – essential in such a high-risk fire zone. Short-term future plans also include several small eco-lodges to provide the full Macedon Ranges accommodation experience complete with stunning sunsets and crisp mornings.

The sculptures on the property came about organically rather than being curated. They are a result of Nonda's friendships with artists, built over many years.

Some of our favourite pieces are actually Nonda's own creations and come from observing the seasons passing across the winery's landscape.

The artwork *Threshold* aligns with the cellar-door entrance and appears as if a gate to the sculpture park. The heavy black concrete layers and Klein blue interior create a shape shifter as the sun passes directly overhead throughout the day. *X sculpture* is the largest work in the collection and is made from the same material used to construct shipping containers. Its bulking form seems to sit so lightly on its concrete base at two points, combining the strength and lightness of a dancer.

Each work appears so differently in the landscape. However, when reading about each you come to realise there is a theme tying them together, and each piece speaks in some way to the environment and conservation.

After you have enjoyed the artworks, it's time to visit the modern cellar door, seemingly colour coded to the large-scale abstract paintings by artist James Clayden, and accessible via a vine-covered pergola. Guests can sit at the circular marble bar to taste estate wines or lounge on the bright couches and try items off the cellar-door menu, including oysters with Mount Monument Riesling Mignonette (yes, yes, I know we were here for a picnic!). Behind this area is the 60-plus seat restaurant overlooking the vines and east towards the township of Romsey.

A relatively high altitude of 630m makes it one of the coolest climates in Australia in which to grow grapes and produce wine. Thankfully, winemaker Ben Ranken is no stranger to producing wine in such a tricky environment. His own vineyard, Wilimee Wines, is located less than half an hour away and he is a lineal descendant of George Rankin who planted some of the first vines in Australia in 1841.

Mount Monument is one of those 'come for a picnic amongst the sculptures but then order oysters and a case of wine to take home' sort of occasions that are a common weekend experience, for us at least.

ANTI-GRAVITY HILL

Okay, bear with us. We are not just getting desperate for ideas and making stuff up now.

If you drive east from Mount Monument winery along Romsey Rd and take a right at Straws Ln, you will find yourself on the legendary Anti-Gravity Hill.

Due to the contours of the surrounding landscape, it appears as if you are driving uphill, however you are actually on a downhill descent. You can witness the illusion yourself by either stopping (near the farm gate of 95 Straw Ln is a good spot) and putting the car in neutral, or pulling over and using the rolling bottled water method (please be aware of any oncoming traffic, obviously). It really is disconcerting to find the car or water bottle rolling uphill and one wonders if there actually IS a military base conducting paranormal experiments nearby!

Apparently, there are only three other known locations in Australia with this same illusion: Ororoo in the mid-north region of SA and two in NSW at Moonbi north of Tamworth and Bowen Mountain at the foothills of the Blue Mountains.

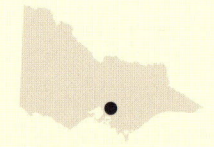

#ONEHOUROUT

Chojo Feature Trees Gallery and Nursery

JAY DILLON

Sassafras, or Sass to the locals, has been a well-known destination for horticulture enthusiasts for decades. The little village boasts a series of quaint, ye-olde-worlde tourist stops nestled within the Dandenong Ranges, and is most famous for the lush, bright green ferns of Sherbrooke and Emerald forests. But there's another secret garden hiding away in this little hamlet, one whose origins could not be further from the English village influence that surrounds it.

Canadian-born Jeff Barry has been practising bonsai design, and helping others through workshops and maintenance services, at this site since 2013 and is revered Australia-wide by enthusiasts, novices and serious collectors alike. Jeff originally travelled to Australia to work for Melbourne-based Maton guitars – another pursuit anchored in artistic tradition – but before he even got his foot in the door there, his interest in little trees had gone from hobby to serious study, and thus his bonsai business was born.

Working under the guidance of craft masters such as Hirotoshi Saito and Peter Adams when they toured Australia, Jeff learned wiring skills and other hands-on techniques via their expert tutelage, and has grown this knowledge into his full-time professional pursuit.

We first noticed the distinctive bright orange Tori gate of Chojo when we were on our way to visit neighbouring Proserpina Bakehouse (which has since moved 2km up the road). Armed with freshly baked batons of sourdough, we ventured along the crunchy stone path into the display gallery that features smaller pieces and custom pots. Another gate took us out into the nursery and gardens; our walking pace naturally slowed to a meander and our eyes began to subconsciously be drawn to the elements that make up each of the bonsai.

Bonsai are miniature living artworks that elicit a response of fascination – much like any other painting or sculpture – and a need to understand the story that sits behind

each piece. This storytelling element is really what gets the Chojo team going when they stop to chat with visitors, and if we didn't understand the evocative drama of nature when we first arrived, we most certainly had our eyes opened to it viewing this tranquil space via Jeff's passionate lens.

Some of the pieces in the Chojo Feature Collection are over a century old and can carry price tags into the thousands. But as with any creative practice, you have to start somewhere, so a small $50 sapling and some basic tools can be picked up in the shop. There are also full-day beginner bonsai workshops run on-site monthly.

As Chojo heads into its second decade, Jeff is particularly excited to be focusing on ceramic collaborations with local artists to produce the perfect pot for each piece. This process takes years in itself, with each tree needing time to grow and inform the artist of how it needs to be housed. Bonsai literally translates to 'tree in tray', so patiently waiting for nature to inform his art is also one of Jeff's unique skills.

GET SASSY

Just like all the towns in the Dandenong Ranges, there are some seriously quirky stores in Sassafras. We don't want to ruin the joy of discovery, so we will leave it to you to wander around the galleries, teahouses and clothing shops. It would, however, be remiss of us to not encourage you to take the 2min-drive up the road to **Proserpina Bakehouse** for their mind-blowing Scaccia, a Sicilian flatbread stuffed with lashings of pastrami, prosciutto or roast veg.

#ONEHOUROUT

Boom Gallery

JAY DILLON

To most Geelong locals, there's nothing particularly 'new' about Newtown, and considering its cultural epicentre – Boom – opened in 2011, we can kind of understand that perspective. But as regular out-of-town visitors to Rutland St, what we've observed, and specifically make the journey to appreciate, is the constantly renewed sense of energy and innovation that the Boom team brings to their ever-expanding physical gallery and studio spaces spread throughout the old wool mill and surrounding buildings like some kind of creative triffid.

For a start, there are *monthly* exhibitions at either Boom Gallery or Big Boom, showcasing contemporary art and design from painting to ceramics, textiles to multimedia and jewellery to furniture. The works may be from established local artists, the hottest interstate 'names' or an emerging international star, and *not* looking at the website before heading off is part of the fun for us – because we never know just what we might see.

It would be easy for a place like Boom to come across as pretentious but, instead, it is a welcoming and warm space that makes you feel completely comfortable – even if you know nothing about art and are drawn from room to room on aesthetic alone.

The vibe is achieved by combining good old-fashioned regional friendliness with a publicly accessible stockroom, a design gallery (that's art-speak for 'shop'), a cafe hosted by sourdough bagel experts **Brother Lawrence**, and a raft of artist studios, whose occupants are always up for a chat and the opportunity to sell you some of their wares or even coax you into taking a class.

Such a behind-the-curtain approach and lack of pomp makes Boom a destination that goes far beyond spot-lit walls; it's for coffee consumption, all-day brekkies, affordable art, inspiration, collaboration, shopping, space hire, socialising, co-working and no doubt more as soon as the next lease becomes available for the group to snap up.

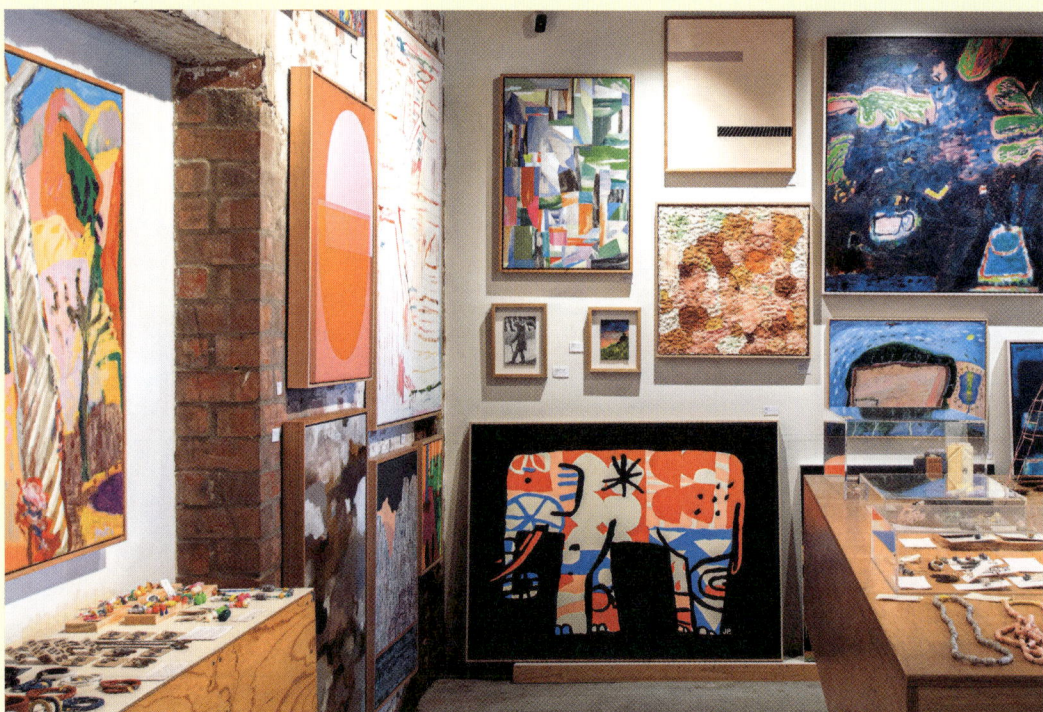

110   UNDISCOVERED VICTORIA

EVERYBODY LOVES GOOD NEIGHBOURS

Once the full Boom experience has been exhausted, we love to wander the rest of Rutland St and take in the other retailers and artisans who've been clever enough to piggyback on their neighbour's success at enticing visitors. Expect to find other smaller creative collectives, plants, fresh flowers, vintage and restoration studios, sustainable clothing, shoes and homewares and a sprinkling of service-based businesses that have transformed the surrounding warehouses into salons and treatment rooms.

BOOKENDING BOOM

If you've got more time to spare, head along Pakington St to turn your Boom visit into a full-day itinerary. Every nook and cranny is crammed with businesses wanting a piece of the Pako action. This is Geelong's shopping strip of both independent labels and chain stores and there are lots of gems here. There are two sections: the Newtown 'river end' closest to Boom Gallery with cafes, boutiques and the beautiful **Peony & Weasel Flower Co** for seasonal flowers and gorgeous gifts, and the West Geelong end with the food market of **Geelong Fresh Foods**, among many other shops and cafes. A fun game to play on Pako is 'spot the typography', to guess how long a place has been open – even the charcoal chicken shop takes visual merchandising and branding seriously at this end of town.

If you're early enough, grab a sanger from **Rossco's**, a tiny, hole-in-the-wall, takeaway-only cafe just past the corner of Hope St, that's (in)famous for selling out way before lunchtime.

If you'd rather dine in, **Box Office** can be found on the corner of Preston and Pako. Owner Mark is a Geelong boy; he loves local produce and knows that if you open early, close late and welcome kids and dogs you'll never not be busy, even if your cafe is in a shipping container.

For somewhere refined for the evening, **Tulip** is a hatted restaurant that absolutely nails casual-service-meets-contemporary-fine-dining, and the only gripe here is that they're closed on Sunday. Be sure to book this one; we learned the hard way.

#FOURANDAHALFHOURSOUT

Australian Pinball Museum

DELLARAM VREELAND

This may very well take the gong as Australia's most unassuming museum, but don't let that deter you from visiting this most eccentric of tourist attractions.

Located in the township of Nhill (don't let that deter you either; there is much to discover in dear old Nhill), just off the Western Hwy en route to Adelaide/Tarndanya, the Australian Pinball Museum is tucked away beside the retro Oasis Motel (*see* p.115).

Housing dozens of pinball machines (plus some arcade favourites) spanning 90 years, most of which are available to play, the museum is Australia's largest public showcase of pinballs and features memorabilia including fliers, posters, autographed art, print media and a whole heap of merch lining its brick-laden walls. The museum also keeps a record of high scores, so you can really get your game on and prove yourself to the rest of the country. Well, those travelling through Nhill anyway.

The museum entrance has been designed to look somewhat like a pinball, with two large white flippers and pop bumpers either side of the doorway. The owners will jovially greet you upon arrival, ready to help with anything you might need. Upon entering, you'll find yourself enveloped in a sea of light, sound and nostalgic wonder. Our family was instantly in a trance, and the kids had a great time deciding which machines they wanted to play – Star Wars and Wonder Boy among the most popular choices.

Each machine costs $1 to play so it's a super-cheap thrill, especially if you've been on the road for hours. Since the machines hail from a wide range of eras, they are hugely varied in their design and aesthetic – electromechanical, solid state, dot-matrix-display and LCD – so not only is the experience an interactive one, it's informative and just downright fascinating. Like stepping in a time machine. For real.

The museum is open right up until 9pm every day.

WHEN YOU'RE ALL GAMED OUT

If you do choose to stay overnight in Nhill, the **Oasis Motel** is a nostalgic choice and has excellent reviews. It was one of the first motels built in Australia during a time when roadside accommodation was all the rage (although they are enjoying a renaissance now). Guests receive a complimentary continental brekky, and you have easy access to the museum. Enjoy the mid-century vibes that ooze throughout, and soak up the warm hospitality that can only be experienced in a country Victorian roadside motor inn.

There's something we love about those quirky destinations that will never appear on the cover of a glossy travel magazine, yet have a certain *je ne sais quoi*. The Pinball Museum and Oasis Motel are among those places.

EXPLORE THE DUNES

Discover the diverse landscapes and the stunning flora and fauna of Western Victoria at **Little Desert National Park**. It's on the Traditional Land of the Wotjobaluk People and a record of their culture, including stone tools, scarred trees and shell middens, has been found here. Located about a half-hour's drive from Nhill, the park has a number of campgrounds nestled by the Wimmera River where you can find repose among the river red gums and wake to the sound of birdsong. With multiple walking trails through the rolling desert dunes, an abundance of native wildflowers during the early summer and late winter, and numerous 4WD tracks, this national park is definitely one for thrillseekers.

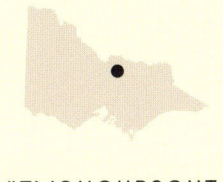

#TWOHOURSOUT

Shepparton Art Museum

DELLARAM VREELAND

We like to think of ourselves as cultured types. Those who take utmost pleasure in traversing the length and breadth of our state to seek out those experiences that explore customs, conversations and art in bold, innovative and creative ways.

The Shepparton Art Museum (SAM) would have to be one of our most favourite cultural institutions in regional Victoria. Overlooking Victoria Park Lake, its stately structure stands proud amongst the eucalypts on Yorta Yorta Country, immediately beckoning visitors to explore what lies within.

The multimillion-dollar, five-level museum officially opened the doors of its new building in late 2021, and features a cafe, children's gallery, shop and library, and also houses the Kaiela Arts Aboriginal art centre and gallery on its ground floor. SAM is probably best known for its dedication to ceramic works, as well as its growing collection of Aboriginal and Torres Strait Islander art.

The museum holds the most significant collection of historic and contemporary Australian ceramics in regional Australia and its collection continues to grow through the acquisitive ceramic awards the Sidney Myer Fund Australian Ceramic Award and the Indigenous Ceramic Award. As lovers of ceramics, we found ourselves in a very happy place, as you can imagine. Such quirky, colourful and whimsical creations to behold!

We were also particularly moved by how profoundly First Nations artists are respected, celebrated and acknowledged within the space. During our visit, the museum was hosting the Fourth National Indigenous Triennial – bringing together commissioned work from First Nations artists across Australia and revealing how ceremony is at the nexus of Country, culture and community. Kaiela Arts also showcased an inspiring exhibition titled *Who We Are*, with works that aimed to nurture, sustain and celebrate First Nations identities. This commitment towards First Nations art is part of SAM's underlying ethos and ensures we can all enrich our understanding of Traditional culture and art.

118   UNDISCOVERED VICTORIA

The kids got a kick out of the specially tailored arts trail. We explored the different spaces, harnessed our inner artist and really unleashed the culture vultures within. Whether you consider yourself an art enthusiast or not, this contemporary museum will have you in awe from the moment you set eyes on its rust-panelled walls.

HOT TIP

Pack a picnic lunch and find your spot amongst the gum trees by Victoria Park Lake with the museum as your backdrop and the lake as your view. Watch as the kids scooter around the park tracks (Shepparton's amazing skate park is also nearby and it is epic, to say the least), or set off on your own afternoon stroll to see what natural wonders you can discover. And while you're in Shepparton, visit the Australian Botanic Gardens (*see* p.148) and the thousands of cars, bikes and dresses at MOVE (*see* p.123).

WHERE WE ART

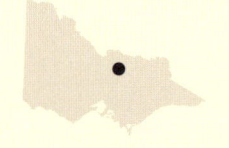

#TWOANDAHALFHOURSOUT

Secret Garden Gigs

JAY DILLON

Music producers Jamie Lea and Hugh Drum were eager to stop the constant drain of local talent from the Goulburn Valley to Melbourne's vibrant live music scene; the duo's brainchild has instead created a unique space for music lovers to connect with homegrown talent. Secret Garden Gigs aren't your ordinary pub gigs though; both the performing acts and the location are kept secret, only revealed to each ticket holder via an email 'love letter' on the morning of the show. Throughout the summer months, the SGG faithful are invited to throw out a picnic rug for a musical sermon that can range from acoustic storytellers to toe-tapping big band ensembles.

When Jamie and Hugh started out nine years ago, they tapped into their network of friends and family with beautiful big backyards to host the events. These days, potential hosts hold events extending well outside the Goulburn Valley. The summer festival gigs mostly sell out just through subscribers to the mailing list, leaving town locals sometimes confused as to who all these new visitors are.

One of the original Secret Garden Gig locations was the old Dookie Quarry. It is a testament to the production skills and dogged determination of Jamie and Hugh that they were able to turn a disused quarry with no power, no water and virtually no infrastructure into a magical mini-musical love fest. The Dookie Quarry event was so popular that it has become its own standalone event – each December 'Grounded' serves as the summer opening event of the Secret Garden Gigs season.

To keep the music flowing in winter, Jamie and Hugh host Winter Sessions in the cosy warmth of the old town halls dotted across the region. When the Winter Sessions rolls into town, the trestle tables and raffle wheel are set aside for a full audio and lightning system and a vintage themed backdrop for the line-up.

Over the nine years of running these events, the duo have established themselves firmly in the local music industry and are often the first port of call for young artists ready to perform outside of the bedroom, as well as more established artists who return home after making their name elsewhere.

#TWOHOURSOUT

MOVE

RICHARD CORNISH

It is one of the largest collections of motor vehicles in the world, filling a whopping 10,000 square metres of a massive purpose-built industrial building in Shepparton's southern suburb of Kialla. MOVE stands for Museum of Vehicle Evolution and is a co-operative of different collections brought together under one gigantic roof. It houses the Furphy collection, over 50 prime movers, 200 bikes, hundreds of privately owned cars and a collection representing 200 years of Australian fashion.

The museum doesn't actually own any of the collections, so when it comes to vintage, veteran and desirable collectible vehicles the curators turn over the floor exhibits every three months or so, borrowing from private collectors. So, on one visit we might get excited about a Ford GTHO with connections to Allan Moffat. On our next visit we could be drooling over the gentle curves and tapered rear of an E-Type Jaguar. The curators have excellent relationships with scores of generous collectors around the state who lend their precious vehicles from 1920s Model A Fords to fully specced-up Toranas, meaning there is an ever-moving feast of sexy, hot, rare and ancient cars.

MOVE is also the permanent home to the Garth Wallace Harley Davidson Collection, which showcases a century's worth of fully restored machines from the big, bold and throaty American motorbike maker. The place we make a beeline for is the Kenworth Dealer Pavilion, which features around 50 trucks, buses, and other commercial vehicles of varying ages. The collection also tells the story of migrants who made their way to the Goulburn Valley. Some turned a single truck, taking tomatoes down to Melbourne, into a multimillion-dollar fleet of freight vehicles. The highlight for the kids is the Kenworth truck cabin bolted in front of a screen on which is projected a looping 15min-long movie of a drive around the backroads of Shepparton.

There is also the Farren Collection, one of the most important collections of bikes in the world with more than 200 two-wheelers, some dating from as early as the 1860s. There are tricycles, penny farthings, and even hobby horses.

A Shepparton local collector was Dick Clayton who was obsessed with all things to do with telecommunications. He played a huge part in the local TV and radio industry through the '70s and '80s and collected all manner of TVs, gramophones and telephones. Older visitors will appreciate the full colour range of 1960s single-piece Ericofons with the rotary dial under the mouthpiece.

Another Shepparton legend is the Furphy iron foundry. Today it makes street furniture but in the early 20th century it was famous for mobile iron water tanks – some of which carried water for troops on the front line at Gallipoli. A large section at the back of the museum has been set aside for the Furphy Museum depicting how Furphy and its tanks helped farmers and soldiers alike.

At the rear of the museum, through a vestibule and unsigned door, is the remarkable Loel Thomson Collection – some 7500 dresses, skirts, coats, hats, shoes and other items of women's clothing and some men's outfits. At any one time over 200 pieces are on display with some of the outfits dating back to the mid-1800s.

Set aside a good two hours, minimum, to move your way through MOVE.

WHERE WE ART 125

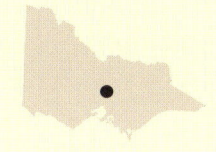

#ONEHOUROUT

Stockroom

JAY DILLON

Strictly speaking, Piper St isn't the main drag in Kyneton, but it is the oldest and most historically intact thoroughfare in town. And within a few compact blocks of its bluestone cobbles and wooden awnings, you'll find a row of some of the best, must-visit contemporary and innovative retailers and eateries this end of the Calder.

Stockroom is one such place. It's a privately owned art space that took up residence in 2010, across the 1000sqm of the old butter factory that's been perched on Piper since the 1850s.

There are two gallery spaces to explore, one dedicated to ceramics – not always functional, but always fascinating pieces – and then a larger, project-based space that could just as easily be showcasing work from someone on the opposite side of the globe by a well-established, recognisable name or a breakthrough talent that you should snap up now.

The directors of Stockroom, Magali Gentric and Jason Waterhouse, are purposeful in their curation, so that even a novice collector or appreciator can afford to purchase some kind of creative piece.

These two collaborators are huge champions of emerging talent, providing the opportunity for group and solo shows every six weeks and supporting artist-in-residency programs that provide free accommodation and exhibitions for creators.

Stockroom is also unabashed about making a delineation between 'artists' and 'makers', which could be a controversial conversation, but one that is explored here with gusto. What's the difference? Well, you'll just have to jump in the car and find out for yourself.

NEED DIGS FOR THE NIGHT?

We love the meticulously renovated, mid-century stylings of the **Kyneton Springs Motel**, whose bright, neon-lit arrow guides you into a nostalgic stay just a little further up Piper St from Stockroom. No two rooms have been styled the same, but they all provide modern amenities, even if the wallpaper is straight out of Graceland and your brekkie arrives through a hatch in the wall.

WHERE WE ART

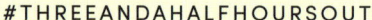

#THREEANDAHALFHOURSOUT

Yeddonba Aboriginal Cultural Site

RICHARD CORNISH

Thylacines roamed Australia for 30 million years. Around 4000 years ago their numbers on the mainland started to decline as dingo numbers grew. By 2000 years ago thylacine had become extinct on the mainland; and when the Europeans arrived they called them Tasmanian tigers. The last Tasmanian tiger died alone in a Hobart zoo in the 1930s. But an ochre image of a thylacine can be seen on the wall of a rock overhang at the base of Mount Pilot. It was painted by ancestors of the local Dhudhuroa People when these striped marsupials were hunting for small prey in the box forest in the granite hills around what today is Beechworth. You can see this remarkable, although faint with age, image along with what looks like a goanna scaling a tree at Yeddonba Aboriginal Cultural Site.

Standing in the bush, looking into the rock face, at animals that lived and died millennia ago, gives an understanding, to a non-Indigenous person, of the enduring connection to Country that exists within First Nations People. Although the images are line drawings, the artist has captured some of the movement and character of the thylacine and goanna.

You can find the site on Yeddonba Rd, off Toveys Rd, off Beechworth–Chiltern Rd, in north-east Victoria. There is a short self-guided walk through the box forest to the site where there is a boardwalk that brings you face to face with the ancient art. It is a site sacred to not only the Dhudhuroa People but also to other local clans who would meet for ceremonies at what is now known as Mount Pilot.

VISIT A FILM SET

A short drive away is the summit of Mount Pilot. Oz cinema students will recognise this bald granite dome as a location used by director Phillippe Mora (son of Mirka) in his 1976 film *Mad Dog Morgan*. It starred Jack Thompson, the late great First Nations actor David Gulpilil and American *Easy Rider* star Dennis Hopper. Hopper is seen riding his horse across the summit, some 550m high, the sun setting over the massive box forest below. You can see the same view on a short walk from the Mount Pilot carpark.

The great bald rock dome is laced with shallow rockpools and on warm days small birds such as wrens and fantails come to drink and bathe in the water. There is supposition that these pools were a water source for the First Nations clans who gathered here.

Where we get close to nature

One of the (countless) things we love about this state of ours is the versatility afforded to us by the land. We love that we can travel every which way, and will be greeted by a diversity of landscapes. There are the rolling green hills of Gippsland, the lush, dense forests of the Dandenongs, the defining outback of the Mallee, the rugged mountains of Gariwerd/Grampians, the ocean views of the Surf Coast and the iconic alpine landscape of the High Country.

We could go on.

In this chapter, we will take you on a tour of some of Victoria's lesser-known natural wonders. You won't find information about famous natural attractions like the Twelve Apostles or Hanging Rock here. Instead, we'll tell you where you can enrich your understanding of First Nations stories at The Flats, Moroopna (*see* p.140) and at Budj Bim Cultural Landscape (*see* p.161). We'll show you where you can go scavenging (without picking!) for a wildflower or two (*see* p.136), and we'll point you in the direction of some of the most outstanding trees and forests you've ever (or never) come across (*see* p.157 and p.145).

During your natural treasure hunt, you're bound to come across a few of our furry friends too, either crossing the road (so be careful while driving), or at some of the national parks and reserves. Say hello to the roos and emus (at Hattah–Kulkyne National Park, *see* p.151), or keep an eye out for the abundant birdlife, wombats and even the odd lizard or two who will surely accompany you along your journey – perfectly rounding off your great Victorian adventure.

Our country is renowned for its rich topography, and Victoria's regions beautifully reflect Australia's expansive landscape. All you need to do is load up the car and go see for yourself.

Let's go exploring!

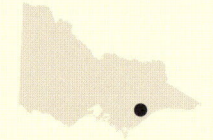

#THREEHOURSOUT

Wildflower spotting, Valencia Creek

DELLARAM VREELAND

Spring may seem like the best time to go wildflower spotting, but these sweet native plants actually flourish in parklands, forests and reserves year-round – all you have to do is look above, around and below.

You're bound to come across wildflowers in any natural setting, so whenever we are travelling we like to keep our eyes peeled for any glimmers of roadside colour. Some wildflowers are endemic, while most species can be discovered all over – growing on tree branches, stemming from lily pads, or peeking through sheaves of grass in forests, parks and along roads.

Victoria boasts many parks and regions that are bursting at the (green) seams with stunning wildflowers. There are those areas where you can find yourself frolicking in a sea of purple hardenbergia, and other places where native peas and yam daisies are scattered throughout the native landscape.

Of all the wondrous natural spaces to explore, we love venturing out to Valencia Creek and surrounds. A peaceful town situated at the foothills of the Great Dividing Range in the Gippsland region, Valencia Creek is nestled within a lush landscape and punctuated by the flowing creek that is its namesake and the Avon River.

As well as featuring many bushwalks, trails and bike tracks, the forest offers the intrepid wayfarer a wildflower treasure hunt of sorts. Venture near and far and see what pretty plants you can spot – donkey and purple-bearded orchids, native peas and daisies to name a few – particularly during the spring and summer seasons. But just a hot tip: many of the roads around this part of town are only accessible by 4WD, so if you plan to head far into the bush (and make the most of your treasure hunt), you will need a strong set of wheels.

We think Valencia Creek is also a pretty special place because, after our ventures, we can find a place of repose by the river's edge and while away rest the of the day surrounded by native Australian bushland and wildlife.

With plenty of places to camp in and around the township, this is one part of the state that is very much worth exploring

TOP Valencia Creek BOTTOM LEFT AND RIGHT Wildflowers in Gariwerd/Grampians

More wildflower wanderings

#ONEANDAHALFHOURSOUT
Slatey Creek

If you're seeking an overdose of wildflower species, Slatey Creek near Creswick will surely indulge your appetite. Native peas, goodenia, drosera and golden spray are just a few of the species that can be found here. The Murnong (yam daisy) can be found here – keep an eye out for its tufted rosette of toothed lanceolate leaves, reminiscent of a dandelion due to its yellow head of florets. Its tuberous roots are edible and were once a staple food source for First Nations people right across Victoria until the flowers were rendered almost extinct with the introduction of sheep and cattle by European settlers.

#THREEHOURSOUT
Gariwerd/Grampians

The Gariwerd/Grampians region is home to a huge variety of emerging wildflowers, including pink and white heath, orchids and blooming tea trees in their natural settings. Wander around the vast bushlands of the mountains and catch a glimpse of the eye-catching flora, or visit in early October for the town hub of Halls Gap's Wildflower Walkabout Weekend.

#ONEANDAHALFHOURSOUT
Woowookarung Regional Park

Located in the regional city of Ballarat, Woowookarung Regional Park is a 641ha park created in 2016 through the ongoing efforts of the local community and its many user groups. Woowookarung means 'place of plenty' in Wadawurrung language, and, as you walk through its meandering tracks and trails, you'll find a plethora of wildflowers including many pea species, such as masses of golden bush-pea or the beautiful hardenbergia sprawling over fallen logs, as well as the dainty native violet or ivy-leaf violet that are very small and grow low to the ground.

#TWOANDAHALFHOURSOUT
The Great Ocean Road

If you're seeking to appreciate wildflowers in a coastal setting, venture to the towns along the Great Ocean Road. Admire banksias, parrot peas and orchids along the Surf Coast Walk, which also crosses the Anglesea heathlands (*see* p.145), near the start of the Great Ocean Road, or traverse heathland in the Bay of Islands Coastal Park where spring wildflowers abound throughout the volcanic landscape of the Tower Hill Wildlife Reserve near the end of the Great Ocean Road. While you're there, Worn Gundidj at Tower Hill allows visitors to experience Country (on a guided tour) through a First Nations lens; the Traditional Owners' oral histories capture the most recent of the volcanic eruptions millennia ago.

OPPOSITE Wildflowers in Gariwerd/Grampians

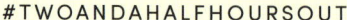

#TWOANDAHALFHOURSOUT

The Flats, Mooroopna

JAY DILLON

On 4 February 1939, Jack Patten led a mass walk-off of some 200 people from Cummeragunja reserve near Barmah. Conditions on the reserve were oppressive and unliveable. The forced isolation imposed by successive governments had degraded the way of life for the mostly Yorta Yorta People who lived at the reserve. In what was the first-ever mass strike of First Nations People in Australia, the people of the reserve crossed to the other side of the river, with many walking over 70km to settle on the flats near Mooroopna.

The Yorta Yorta People have a long association with the site, which flooded regularly and provided a rich source of food like turtles (except for the broad-shelled, long-neck turtle which is a totem) and their eggs, blackfish, cod and birds like swan and crane. Springs near the river flowed with clean crystal-clear water for drinking and keeping food cool. Elders who remember living on The Flats recall a tough but mostly happy existence.

In 1954, when Queen Elizabeth II visited Victoria, she travelled over the bridge that overlooked the Flats where hessian bags were hung to obscure her view of First Peoples camped there, such were the conditions. Many Yorta Yorta People see this as a key part in history, as, after she saw the conditions, action was finally taken to improve living conditions, which was an early precursor to the Rumbalara housing being established.

Today, walking through the Flats with the aid of the good interpretive signage and a mindful stillness, absorbing the story of the people who moved out of oppression to make their home on these river flats, listening to the Traditional cultural stories and acknowledging the darker more recent past create a visceral experience.

There are organised walks that run on an ad-hoc basis, through the Yorta Yorta Nation Aboriginal Corporation. When we were lucky enough to be given a guided tour by Uncle Reuben Baksh, he told us of the story of his mother and grandmother, and how the women would leave town to be here on the river flats to give birth hidden

in the safety of tree hollows because babies were taken at that time under the White Australia Policy. He also tells the stories of the people who made simple but free lives here.

'How do we learn more, gain more understanding, Uncle?'

'Spend more time on Country. Take it in. Listen to the stories. Pass them on.'

It's a simple message, and it's the responsibility of every Australian. It's also a really simple thing to do. Get out of the car, and take a quiet walk on Country. In places like The Flats and Gawa Reserve and Yeddonba. But the message is the same. Spend some time on Country and gain a little understanding.

#ONEHOUROUT

Leadbeater's possum, Yarra Ranges

JAY DILLON

I'm trying to focus on the skyline above, but my mind is preoccupied with the scratching sound near my feet. I had thought lying down on an old log that had fallen to the forest floor would be the best place to position myself. Little did I know it was actually a major thoroughfare for the local residents and I was blocking the way.

Clearly, I'm not too much of an obstacle as the bush rat scrambles upon my ankle and proceeds without a care up the entire length of my body, jumping off at my shoulder, leaving me wide-eyed and breathless as it continues on its way through the ferns.

I'm here with around 30 other volunteers, deep in the water-catchment area of Yarra Ranges National Park. The sun has set behind rows of mountain ash and the forest floor has dropped close to 10°C. I've been positioned next to a 'stag tree,' a dead or old decaying tree that has been identified as a suitable habitat for the Leadbeater's possum (wollert) and other arboreal marsupials like gliders. My job is to spend the next hour taking notes of any creatures I spot coming in and out of the hollows of the one particular tree; noting species, abundance and the time.

I'm not the first person to observe this particular tree. In fact, there's a chance one of the hundreds of people who have observed this same tree also made the mistake of blocking the forest highway. This tree is located in one of 182 sites that are part of a forest survey program that has been running for 40 years and has contributed greatly to the understanding and conservation of the mountain and alpine ash forests. The program is run by Professor David Lindenmayer, AO, and the Australian National University, and unfortunately has documented a serious decline in these types of marsupials, as well as birds and the 120+ year-old stags that are the key to their survival.

This mountain ash forest is part of the Central Highlands of Victoria, covering about 1.1 million hectares, and can be reached in as little as an hour's drive from Melbourne/Naarm. The ecosystem is hugely diverse, changing from dense cool temperate rainforest to cold snow gum woodlands and dry eucalypt forests with a wattle lower storey. For tens of thousands of years, these mountains were the symbiotic living resource for the Gunai/Kurnai, Taungurung and Wurundjeri Peoples, who have maintained an ongoing custodianship with the forests and waters. In more recent times, industrial logging and wildfire have had a huge impact on the forests and the loss of habitat has driven much of the wildlife to extinction.

Earlier, as our group took the drive up into the national park with an urgency to ensure we had plenty of time to set up before dusk, it was clear that everyone in the vehicle was hoping to catch a glimpse of the wollert whilst on the survey. The wollert, with its Disney-esque eyes, was found in fossils in NSW and considered extinct right up until 1961 when it was rediscovered in the forests east of Marysville. It is the only marsupial whose habitat is restricted to the state of Victoria, so it's no wonder that ten years later it was made our faunal emblem.

Wollert live in small colonies of about 12 in hollows found in mountain ash and alpine ash trees that are between 150 and 400 years old. Unfortunately, their habitat is constantly under threat from fire and logging and the species is listed as Critically Endangered (the last conservation status level before Extinct).

Monitoring programs like the one managed by Professor Lindenmayer play an essential role in informing government policy related to the conservation of these forest ecosystems and the species that live within them. Volunteering gives you a wonderful opportunity to experience spectacular nature, while also contributing to crucial research.

WHERE TO SEE A LEADBEATER'S POSSUM

The last Leadbeater's possum in captivity was Kasia, who passed away in the Metro Zoo, Toronto in 2010. The **Healesville Sanctuary** runs a captive breeding program of the genetically distinct lowland Leadbeater's possums in the Yellingbo Nature Reserve, which is not accessible to the public.

To contribute to Professor Lindenmayer's research program, send an email to fses-cle-admin@anu.edu.au and put 'Stagwatch volunteering' in the subject line.

Also consider joining the Great Forest National Park campaign to protect the wollert habitat once and for all. Sign up online (greatforestnationalpark.com.au).

Unique forests

RICHARD CORNISH

Whenever we wander into Victoria's forests we are reminded that the word 'forest' has the same Latin root as the word 'foreign'. They both come from 'foris', meaning outside, or another place.

Victoria's forests are like other worlds. Some are towering mazes of solid eucalypt timber, the canopy dancing in the sky somewhere overhead. Other forests are low, stunted, gnarled trees that hold sand dunes together tenaciously with their hidden roots, their limbs home to goannas and countless tiny birds. Then there are the forests that straddle both sea and land, great ribbons of green mangrove that send up roots above the high-tide mark to breathe while still mostly submerged underwater, home to thousands of crabs that emerge at low tide.

These are the places where you take a glimpse into the life and home of the birds, marsupials, insects, reptiles, plants and fungi that make up these incredibly intricate, interwoven environments.

Sadly, we have lost almost 90 per cent of our forest in Victoria, so what is left is truly precious. Be mindful of this when you travel and do what you can to conserve these special places.

#SIXANDAHALFHOURSOUT
Errinundra Plateau

Up in the hills above Orbost, in far-east Gippsland, is an ancient mountain wonderland. Often cloaked in mist, the forests of the towering shining gums and gnarled mountain plum pines grow amongst a canopy of tree ferns and great expanses of moss-covered rocks. It is one of the last extents of cool-climate rainforest in the world and home to several species of possums and gliders. Perched on the edge of the NSW border, much of the area is covered by national park but, sadly, large sections are still open to logging. Log trucks pose a hazard on the narrow, winding, unmade roads, and visitors need to be wary. There is a thrill, however, being amongst a forest where some of the individual trees are over 1000 years old and measure some 20m in girth. Some *Podocarpus*, or mountain pine, species have been growing here for millions of years, giving parts of the forest an eerie Jurassic feel. The area is generally always wet – the source of seven different rivers – so wear sturdy waterproof boots.

#TWOHOURSOUT
Anglesea Heath

Down the Great Ocean Road, in the low hills around Anglesea, is a 7000ha reserve managed by Parks Victoria, protecting one of the most ecologically diverse landscapes in the country. Here the soil is poor, and the manna gums and stringybarks grow small and stunted, but the conditions are perfect for the native heaths, grass trees, banksias, grasses, and wildflowers that carpet the ground. Well-made paths intersect this country, giving

#ONEHOUROUT
Mangrove forest

One of the most southerly mangrove forests on the planet can be found on the outskirts of the industrial town of Hastings on Western Port on the Mornington Peninsula. Earmarked for development by Premier Henry Bolte in the 1960s, Western Port was to be Victoria's industrial heartland, and this strip of glossy-leafed marine trees bulldozed. However, this important coastal environment survived destruction and is now recognised globally (under the Ramsar Convention) as an essential bird habitat and coastal wetland environment. Join the trail from the marina to the boardwalk that will guide you through the forest and above the high-water mark as the waters of Western Port ebb and flow. At low tide, the muddy sand comes alive with crabs scurrying about under the labyrinth of roots. They are joined by herons, oystercatchers, spoonbills and scores of smaller birds darting about the branches. The walk passes Sandstone Island heading to Jacks Creek. When the tide comes in, so do the fish, and the shallow water under the trees is filled with small fish darting about.

Walking access to the low forest where koalas graze in the treetops and swamp wallabies hop about their solitary trails. Come late winter and spring, the forest floor erupts with life as the wildflowers bloom. Some are tiny greenhood orchids; some are trigger orchids whose petals entrap pollinating insects at the lightest touch; there are orchids with the aroma of chocolate, while some banksia flowers ooze nectar that tastes like honey.

#TWOHOURSOUT
Mountain ash forests

In 1888, to celebrate the Centennial International Exhibition, a reward of 20 guineas was offered to anyone who could locate a tree in Victorian forests taller than 400ft or 122m. The tallest found was 99.4m, and was promptly chopped down and taken to Melbourne/Naarm. Those trees were mountain ash, *Eucalyptus regnans* – meaning 'ruling'. These forest royals are the world's tallest flowering plants. They can still be found in the forests of the Dandenong Ranges, the Otway Ranges and Strzelecki Ranges. Much of the forest today is regrowth after bushfires, but these smooth-barked forest giants are still impressive, standing above the tree ferns and babbling mountain streams. We love the Benwerrin-Mount Sabine Rd, an hour-long drive winding through mountain ash and stringybark forest near Deans Marsh inland from Lorne, and walking the tracks around Sassafras in the Dandenong Ranges. The Grand Strzelecki Track is a network of trails that explores the great forests around Balook between Churchill and Yarram and one of the lesser-known hiking destinations in the state.

#FIVEHOURSOUT
Cabbage trees

Inland from where the Snowy River flows into the sea, an isolated stand of cabbage trees forms an island of subtropical foliage surrounded by eucalypts and banksia forest. This place is Cabbage Tree Creek. The only palm trees to be found growing wild in Victoria, cabbage trees are usually found near the Queensland and NSW coast. An important food and fibre plant for First Nations People, it is thought this Victorian population might have been planted on a trade route. This short 1km walk takes you through the palms, with the glossy fronds clattering in the breeze. We always stop here when driving along the Princes Hwy heading to Mallacoota. If you have a 4WD, you can make the most of the glorious forest tracks that link the Cape Conran Coastal Rd back to the highway.

#FIVEHOURSOUT
Wyperfeld National Park

In the height of summer the Mallee gets hot. Damn hot. The bush is still, and when the storm clouds build it's time to get out, as a single lightning strike can set the forest alight. Mallee trees are very short eucalypt trees, so adapted to fire that they have no trunk, just short straight limbs, no more than 5m tall that grow directly from the root. When winter rains come in from the west, the sand dunes become a blaze of colour with myriad wildflowers and bushes bursting into bloom. One great place to experience the harsh beauty of the Mallee is Wyperfeld National Park in the north-west of the state between Ouyen and Nhill. The tracks on the low sand dunes make for great four-wheel driving through this semi-arid landscape. When the Wimmera River flows into ephemeral Lake Hindmarsh, a chain of lake beds fills, transforming the park. Come for the great camping, birdwatching and night skies.

#FOURHOURSOUT
Banksia forests

Along the far east Gippsland coastline are strips of banksia forest where these silver-leafed trees grow to 20m tall. They spread out along the dunes, some centuries old, creating cool swales where birds and marsupials are protected from the sun and coastal winds. While much was burned in the 2019–20 fires, regrowth and regeneration have seen these beautiful and wild habitats return. Some of the best are at Raymond Island, Cape Conran near Marlo and Croajingolong National Park further east. These forests evolved with fire, and the seed cones need smoke to release their nuts. The branches are home to cockatoos, while antechinus hide under the lower foliage. When in the area, we head to local beekeepers and buy banksia honey, which tastes like bananas cooked in brown sugar. Check ahead of travel to ensure Croajingolong National Park is fully open.

RIGHT AND OPPOSITE Banksia forests, Raymond Island **PREVIOUS** Cabbage trees

#TWOHOURSOUT

Australian Botanic Gardens

JAY DILLON

Put your hands in the air if you fit any of the following categories: nature lover, environmentally aware, recycler, re-user, lover of anything to do with sustainability. Well, that pretty much sums up the team here at OHO, so you can imagine how intrigued we were to hear about a botanic garden built entirely on top of a landfill site.

You read that correctly. A botanic garden, set across a 25ha landfill site and not a rose garden in sight. It's been a long time coming because no one has done this before and after hearing the story about how this garden came about, we realise why.

For years the Shepparton tip had grown into a huge mountain of waste, until it was finally shut down by the Environment Protection Authority (EPA) and the mound capped by the local council. Eventually, a masterplan was developed with input by a community committee. The initial focus was on the huge mound, since renamed Honeysuckle Rise after a rare local banksia, with terracing added for planting out natives. Through community engagement the masterplan expanded to include themed gardens that both rehabilitate the land and draw on the cultural, historical and environmental characteristics of the Goulburn Valley. The infrastructure works included remodelling of the floodway into life-giving wetlands that are flooded each year by the nearby Goulburn and Broken rivers.

Honeysuckle Rise takes in a panoramic view of the Shepparton area, and we recommend avoiding the heat of the day to visit, and taking in the view across the city at sunrise or sunset. It's built with recycled materials and planted out masterfully with Australian native plants. The landscape is still a work in progress, but how often do you get to see the beginning of something so significant?

There is a range of cycling and walking paths to explore, from the river paths to the Honeysuckle Track. All are accessible and vary in length. There are also themed gardens around the park, like the Refugee Garden, which celebrates the 'melting-pot' that is created by the welcoming of refugees to the region, and the Children's Garden, which promotes play and sensory experiences.

A new section in development is dedicated to the land management practices of the Yorta Yorta People before European settlement and will be planted out to represent the four bioregions of the Goulburn Valley. It is hoped that this will also include a First Nations–led education program.

Victoria has some excellent botanic gardens, many of which were the work of the excessively fidgety green thumbs of William Guilfoyle (Hamilton, Colac and of course the Royal Botanic Gardens in Melbourne/Naarm). These gardens are indisputably stunning, with their glittering lakes, bright green lawns and collection of significant species from around the world. However, we love that the Australian Botanic Gardens looks internally rather than externally. It recognises the importance of indigenous species and the intrinsic beauty in the rough-and-ready native flora, and takes inspiration from the culture and history of the region.

Not bad for an old tip!

#FIVEANDAHALFHOURSOUT

Hattah-Kulkyne National Park

RICHARD CORNISH

Hattah-Kulkyne in Victoria's north-west is as close as we get to outback in Victoria without crossing the border. Up here in the Mallee the horizons are massive, the colours kaleidoscopic and the night skies jet black and punctuated with a billion blazing points of lights. Visiting this beautiful part of the world has been part of an annual pilgrimage. We dine at Stefano's restaurant in Mildura and slowly drive back through Hattah, meandering along sandy tracks through the forest and around the glittering lakes.

Hattah-Kulkyne National Park covers some 48,000ha of country, and is the Traditional home of the Latje Latje People. Hattah-Kulkyne includes many culturally significant sites, including scar trees where canoes and shields were cut from bark generations ago, as well as middens.

The park consists of a strip that runs north–south adjacent to a loop in the Murray River as it heads north from the town of Liparoo. Then there is a larger strip running adjacent to the Calder Hwy. It's about 450km north of Melbourne/Naarm, 75km south of Mildura.

Much of the park is covered in rolling red and yellow sand dunes cloaked in mallee gum and Murray pine. Around the waterways is a thin ribbon of ancient river red gums. The lakes are fed by creeks leading to the Murray River and rise and fall depending on the flow of the river, flooding every several years. The 2022 floods were dramatic and damaged infrastructure that could still take some time to repair. These vast bodies of freshwater in the middle of a quite arid landscape create valuable habitat to huge numbers of birds,

and large parts of the park have been recognised by the Ramsar Convention, the international treaty on wetland bird habitat. The shorelines of the lakes are often lined with red-capped plovers, while the endangered Mallee emu-wren can be seen in the grasses nearby.

In the sand dunes, under the broad spreading Mallee gums, are the nests of Mallee fowl. About the size of a large skinny turkey, these quirky birds make large nests by scraping up sand and leaves to make mounds, some 1.5m high and 4m across. In the centre they lay their eggs which they incubate with the heat generated by rotting leaves and the radiant warmth of the sun. Hunting, feral animals and loss of habitat have reduced the number of birds to a point where they are now vulnerable. But to a quiet bushwalker they are not an uncommon sight, especially when they take flight on their stubby wings when startled. In the beautiful Murray pine forest, which at times resembles the deserts of Arizona, can be seen pairs of Major Mitchell cockatoos, a beautiful white and dusky pink bird with a Leunig-like curly quiff of feathers. Emus are a common sight, as are roos and wallabies. At night the haunting call of the boobook fills the still air.

There are two campgrounds in the park, a viewing tower, hundreds of kilometres of waterways and 2WD roads. Being dry country, it can get hot during the summer days and cold at night. If camping, bring plenty of water, your own firewood, a good tent or swag, a sleeping bag, sturdy walking boots and spend a night or two gazing into the endless sky. Sunsets can be extraordinary, lighting the whole forest with different hues that change from orange to red to mauve.

WHERE WE GET CLOSE TO NATURE

#ONEANDAHALFHOURSOUT

Weedy sea dragons, Flinders Pier

RICHARD CORNISH

One of the easiest and most accessible underwater adventures in the state is under the pier at Flinders on Western Port on the Mornington Peninsula. Here live several families of leafy sea dragons that move about the pylons and under the pier.

These beautiful and harmless little creatures are close relatives of seahorses and move slowly through the water, blending into the seaweed growing on the old wooden pylons and weedy sea floor with their intricate camouflage. Green, brown and purple, their only protection are small spikes and seaweed-like fins that render them invisible to predators when they snuggle into the slowly waving seaweed.

You can probably gather that we have a soft spot for these gorgeous little critters. So does Sir David Attenborough. It was 2021 when he found out that the historic Flinders Pier was under threat from being demolished by the government, and he joined the local activists in petitioning the government to save the pier. The leafy

sea dragons have made a home amongst the seaweed growing on the old timber supports, and removing them would have meant an end to the colony. Thankfully the pier was saved and so too the dragons.

You just need goggles, snorkel and flippers and perhaps a wetsuit in cooler months. There are various ladders reaching from sea level to the pier boardwalk, or you can swim out from the shore or dive in on off the deck of the pier (check tides, depth and for submerged rocks and other obstacles beforehand). The water is about 3 to 4m deep. Making the pier home are countless fish, calamari and large eagle rays, their wingspan of about 1.5m makes them a formidable dark shape in the water when you're snorkelling several metres underwater.

There is no need to swim out to the deeper water. That said, the snorkel under the pylons of the pier, from shore to the end some 250m away, is quite an interesting trip watching the species of seaweed and fish change the deeper the water gets. While snorkelling is a relatively safe pastime, Flinders Pier is exposed to sea swell and the beach is not patrolled, so watch the weather and take it safe.

The mouth to Western Port is wide and the water flowing in from Bass Strait keeps the water cool, especially in winter. This makes late summer and early autumn the warmest and calmest times of the year and the perfect time to plan a trip down to Flinders Pier.

While you're in Flinders, buy fresh or cooked mussels from **Flinders Mussels** or the **La Conchilia food** van (*see* p.70).

WHERE WE GET CLOSE TO NATURE

Significant trees

RICHARD CORNISH

We have always been enthralled by spectacular trees. From an early age, they have played a big part in our growing up, from the trees we climbed, the trees we made cubbies under, the trees that fed us, and the trees that died and ended up warming us in the fireplace. Trees grew in significance as we grew older and as we read about magic faraway trees, tall trees, small trees, gnarled trees and ancient trees. Dotted around the state, unique trees and stands of trees draw tree lovers. Some are simply old and big. Some are the only ones you'll find in the world. Others have deep cultural and spiritual significance to First Nations People. Once you visit a significant tree, it becomes like a friend in a distant place. Trees occupy a place in your mind, and you often have the hankering to see them to ensure they are thriving and doing well.

#ONEANDAHALFHOURSOUT

Ballarat's Avenue of Honour

Ballarat

Lined up on either side of the old Western Hwy are nearly 4000 elms, oaks and other European trees planted over a hundred years ago. Each tree represents the 3912 men and women from Ballarat and surrounds who fought and served in World War I. There are 528 trees that mark locals who died. The trees were planted over several years from 1917 and paid for by employees of the Lucas Clothing Factory, who made dolls from fabric scraps and sold them to raise funds. The avenue starts on the edge of Ballarat on Sturt St and continues some 22km toward Beaufort. The first living war memorial of its kind in the world, today it's a shady drive in summer and a stark reminder in winter, when the trees lose their leaves, of what was meant to be the 'war to end all wars'.

#NOTEVENONEHOUROUT

River red gum

Melbourne/Naarm

For 800 years, the people of the Boon Wurrung/Bunurong tribe have sat under a river red gum that was part of an open woodland that gave way to wetlands nearby, the perfect place to hunt for eel, turtle, freshwater blackfish, mussels and waterbird eggs. That wetland is now Albert Park Lake in Melbourne/Naarm, and that tree now stands on the edge of St Kilda's Junction oval and is passed by thousands of motorists each day. It is one of several river red gums important to local First Nations People. When riding along the Yarra River/Birrarung, we stop and pay our respects to the Corroboree Tree on the edge of Burnley Oval, once an important cultural meeting place. There is also a scar tree at Yarra Bank Reserve at Denham St in Hawthorn, which remains important to the Wurundjeri People.

#TWOHOURSOUT

Ada Tree

Ada

At 300 years old, the Ada Tree is a survivor. The 75m-tall tree is a mountain ash, beautifully described botanically as *Eucalyptus regnans* – regnans being Latin for 'ruling'. We like to simply call her Ada. Ada can be found on a track in the Yarra Ranges at Ada, east of Powelltown. The tallest flowering plant in the world, some of Ada's sisters have been measured at over 100m. Most were cut down in the late 1800s. Those that survived were burned in the devastating 1939 bushfire. The 40min walk is stunning, with towering tree ferns and, above them, the stags of remnant mountain ash that are home to sugar gliders, greater gliders, and scores of different birds. There are patches of wet rainforest and a boardwalk to keep you above the leeches. When you come to

Ada, she is a stunning example of a tall tree, with a massive girth supported by the base of the trunk, forming buttresses like a living Notre Dame.

#TWOHOURSOUT
The Big Tree
Guildford

In the little town of Guildford, halfway between Castlemaine and Daylesford, is a giant, sprawling river red gum called The Big Tree. Locals don't know how old it is, but some say it is possible it was a sapling when the Normans invaded England. It is 30m high, and its canopy spreads over 34m. Great limbs, the diameter wider than a big man's chest, have recently broken off, revealing chambers big enough to crawl through. It is full of life with a beehive high up, the sound of limb rubbing on limb, the rustle of the wind through the leaves and the buzz of insects coming to feast on nectar in the flowers and birds coming to feed on the insects. In summer, we visit The Big Tree on the way back from swimming in the Loddon River at Vaughan Springs (*see* p.9). In winter, we combine a visit to our old eucalypt mate before we head to a counter tea by the fire at the **Guildford Family Hotel**.

#TWOHOURSOUT
The English oak
Castlemaine

Castlemaine is one of our favourite places in autumn to run through the piles of fallen leaves from the scores of oaks, elms, cedars, and maples planted through the gardens. The Botanic Gardens was gazetted in 1860 and a small English oak was planted in 1863 to celebrate the marriage of Albert Edward, Prince of Wales, to Alexandra of Denmark. Now 160 years later, that oak is 22m tall, spreading out with a limb span of 35m. This majestic tree offers cool respite in summer, a glorious cloak of yellow and orange by the autumnal equinox, and a beautiful twisted silhouette against the winter sky.

#THREEHOURSOUT
Scar Tree, Boort
Lake Boort

There is an ancient river red gum near the banks of Lake Boort near Myrong Beach. Dead for years, it bears a large elliptical scar around its fat belly-like trunk. Before colonisation this is where a member of the Yung Balug clan of the Dja Dja Wurrung People cut out a coolamon: a fire-cured and curved piece of bark to carry water, food, ochre, even infants. It is one of over 500 like trees around Lake Boort and surrounds, and one of 2000 in the district, making it the largest collection of First Nations scar trees on the planet. There are trees with footholds axed into the trunk where the young men would have climbed the tree hunting possums or eggs and even scars where burls have been removed. These great dome-shaped growths were hollowed out, most likely through fire, to make water containers. A 45min walking track around the smaller Little Boort Lake reveals the remains of First Nations' clay ovens: clay balls baked to stone-like hardness to use in underground cooking pits. The wealth of easily accessible artefacts is mind blowing in this little town and we always book ahead to make sure we meet up with Paul Haw who runs the Yung Balug Museum. He has an exceptional collection of photographs and pre-colonial tools used by the Traditional Owners of this area 200km north-west of Melbourne/Naarm.

TOP LEFT AND RIGHT The Big Tree
BOTTOM Ballarat's Avenue of Honour
PREVIOUS The English Oak

WHERE WE GET CLOSE TO NATURE

#FOURHOURSOUT

Budj Bim Cultural Landscape

RICHARD CORNISH

Recognised by UNESCO in 2019, over 6000 years old and just a 40min drive from Port Fairy and near Heywood, Budj Bim Cultural Landscape is what remains of a vast series of stone villages built on the edge of an intricate system of water channels and weirs by the Gunditjmara People from about 4000BC until colonisation. The water system was built around a large expanse of water, named Lake Condah by settlers, to trap kooyang or the southern short-finned eel. The lake was drained in the middle of the 20th century.

Since time immemorial, this vast and powerfully rugged place has been carefully and quietly nurtured by the Gunditjmara locals. Despite being unable to practice Traditional cultural traditions due to restrictive and oppressive government policies

WHERE WE GET CLOSE TO NATURE

across the 19th and 20th centuries, Traditional Owners have carefully returned the drained lake to close to its original levels. The oral histories of Traditional Owners describing the volcanic activity in the region that led to the formation of significant geographic features has been dated by volcanologists and geologists at more than 27,000 years old. The Gunditjmara People lived along the water system here in permanent stone huts, and trapped, smoked and traded kooyang for thousands of years.

In 2022, after decades of planning and working with the local community, the Gunditjmara People opened their sacred landscape up to visitors. Foremost they opened the doors to Tae Rak Aquaculture Centre. This $2 million visitor centre complex has a cafe and interpretative area facilities that will allow local Gunditjmara People to once again harvest, process and smoke eels, as they have done for thousands of years, but now in a state-of-the-art facility. Open Wednesday to Sunday, it looks out over the lake and offers visitors a chance to taste real smoked short-finned eel in a manner of delicious ways, including in arancini or as part of a tasting plate with eel pâté, deep-fried smoked eel skin, and smoked eel on crackers plus preserves. There are other less eel-oriented dishes that still have a focus on native Australian ingredients, such as mussels in tomato chilli broth and lemon myrtle scones with cream and jam. The food at Tae Rak has been of a high standard every time we have visited.

The tours are a true eye-opener. Although they are run by the younger members of the local Gunditjmara People, it seems you are in the company of old souls. The wisdom, knowledge and respect for Country and others they possess is both remarkable and admirable. On the 2hr tour, you are taken from the visitor information centre to the start of the lava flows that created Lake Condah and told some of the stories around the area. We learned that Budj Bim (known as Mount Eccles to colonials), the volcano that dominates the skyline, erupted around 27,000 years ago, spewing red-hot lava for scores of kilometres and forming Lake Condah. Budj Bim was one of four giants that arrived in this part of Australia. Budj Bim became a volcano and spat out teeth, or the giant lava rocks that dominate the landscape. It is an unfathomably moving place with hollow lava tubes with a history so ancient, you can feel it on your skin.

A stone axe found buried beneath the lava flow by archaeologists indicates that humans have been in this area since before the eruption. That the Gunditjmara People are still telling the story of the eruption 37,000 years later is a likely candidate for the oldest story still being told on the planet.

The half-day tour includes these stories and also allows time to delve deeper into this maze-like structure of ancient reservoirs, channels and village sites. It took us to an ancient smoking tree, a hollowed-out manna gum under which scientists

Guide Braydon Saunders

have detected amounts of eel fat, rendered from eels as they were smoked to preserve them for trade. The tour also takes in old weirs and a dam where kooyang were trapped and held. We learned that hydrologists who studied the channels saw that the water flow could be turned on or off by simply moving a rock that nestled tightly into the channel. The canals themselves were hewn into the lava by building fires on the rock and then shattering it by pouring on cold water.

The full-day tour immerses you in the Gunditjmara cultural perspective. You visit a volcano hollowed out by a blast and now infilled by a deep crater lake. When the guides take you to visit their weirs, stone huts and celestial calendar site and you share a delicious morning tea and lunch – including eel – you begin to see the world through the eyes of the Gunditjmara People. The eel story is just the beginning.

Where we eat

We know full well that people travel with their stomachs, and by people we mean us. Most of the itineraries we conjure up for ourselves are planned around the culinary destinations we've gotten wind of, where we can stop off for some good old-fashioned country grub – and some not-so-old-fashioned eats.

The most compelling reason to visit Victoria's regional eateries is because of the literal paddock-to-plate experience we are lucky enough to be offered. The dishes forged in these establishments – whether it's the local cafe or high-end restaurant – showcase the finest fare sourced from surrounding farmers and producers. Take for example Bar Midland in Castlemaine (see p.180), whose sustainable practices lend themselves to an impressive menu of food either locally grown or harvested in Victoria.

Get ready to send your senses astir as you rummage through the next few pages and peruse the delectable offerings that you never knew existed in this vast state of ours. From the kerbside gourmet sanga shop that is Mortadeli (see p.186), to the fine-dining, intimate experience of Greasy Zoe's (see p. 174), and the authentic Turkish food of Babil at Oddfellows (see p.177), we have a smorgasboard selection of gastronomic delights for you to pore over.

It's really no exaggeration when we say country chefs are using ingredients from their very own backyards, so you can bet your bottom dollar your experience will be characterised by freshness, wholesomeness and a celebration of country Victoria.

Check if you need to book ahead before you go exploring as many of these foodie stops – like most venues since the pandemic – need to plan for staff and supplies in advance.

So pens a'ready. It's time to start planning your gastronomic getaways.

Let's go dining!

#THREEANDAHALFHOURSOUT

The Long Paddock

RICHARD CORNISH

The sun rises over the Mitchell River valley, flooding the escarpment with rosy pink light. Perched on top, near the old butcher shop and across the road from the long-gone garage, is Lindenow's old town bakery. This was once the heart and soul of this little country town and farming community near Bairnsdale, 330km east of Melbourne/Naarm. It is now called The Long Paddock, a cafe/restaurant full of mismatched mid-century furniture warmed by the old Scotch oven that is now used to roast meats and bake cakes.

It is owned by husband-and-wife chefs Anton Eisenmenger and Tanya Bertino. Between them they have cooked in some of the best restaurants in Australia and around the world. The list includes Ledbury in London and The Botanical and Vue de Monde in Melbourne. A few years back, they left the frantic pace of fine dining in the city and returned to Tanya's home town of Lindenow. At first they thought they might start a business in the regional centre of Bairnsdale, until they took a look at the cafe in Lindenow that was up for sale with that old wood-fired Scotch oven.

The couple decided they wanted to cook the food they grew up with and love. Food to nourish the locals. The menu is as simple as it is beautiful. There could be seasonal dishes such as asparagus served on fresh, house-made curd with a hardboiled egg and breadcrumbs grated over the top, or beef slow-cooked in the wood-fired Scotch. Follow your meal with the well-executed patisserie, such as nut and chocolate cake slathered in ganache, or a perfectly set lemon tart. The shelves are lined with jams and conserves and the benches are groaning with baked goods. And if you only want a sandwich, Anton makes his own corned beef for his excellent corned beef sandwiches.

When we hit the road to visit East Gippsland, we leave early to ensure we arrive here mid-morning, just as the desire for coffee and pastry reaches its peak. While waiting for our brew, we marvel at what a central part of the community the cafe has become, with farming neighbours dropping in excess fruit and vegetables for use in the kitchen. It's a community as warm as the old Scotch at the back of the room.

WHERE WE EAT

#ONEANDAHALFHOURSOUT

Trawool Estate

JAY DILLON

For years we have driven past this Fawlty Towers–like hotel, sitting glumly and alone on the road between Yea and Seymour. Although we are prone to drop into just about any venue with a hope of revealing the undiscovered, in this case there wasn't discernible activity to warrant an exploration. That was until a local family purchased the hotel with the vision to create a 20-room boutique country resort.

The Taungurung name for the area is Traawool, meaning 'wild water' in reference to the fast-flowing Goulburn River that flows and floods the valley. It was renamed Trawool (European settlers often adapted First Nations names) by pastoralists in the early 1900s, and when a train line was built from nearby Tallarook to Yea, the Trawool Valley became quite the destination for walking in nature, boating and fishing.

In the 1970s, Melbourne planners started to discuss the idea of flooding the valley to create a hydro-electric scheme. The locals were having none of it and instead successfully campaigned to have the valley awarded Scenic Classification by the National Trust.

The Trawool Hotel was built where a barge carried passengers across the Goulburn River, and stood for many years as a bit of a dishevelled reminder of a forgotten town.

It took a father-and-son team from Seymour to see the potential for the creation of a destination food and accommodation experience. With no hospitality experience, Wes and Terry Old purchased the building at auction in 2019 and immediately undertook renovations that brought it into line with expectations of the modern visitor, but with respect to its past history and the space it holds in the mind of locals.

It's clear Wes and Terry have put their hearts into the dining experience, with three options from casual to fine dining. After a quick gin in the Granite bar, we head for dinner in Wild Water, which has recently transitioned to modern Italian. The pork for the roast porchetta is sourced locally and the stuffing inside and the salsa verde on top are all made from ingredients grown in the garden beds out front.

We aren't ones to subscribe to the 'only order seafood when you are near the sea' philosophy because ... hello refrigerated trucks! What's more important is the Merimbula appellation graded oysters are shucked at point of order and the pan-fried barramundi is perfectly cooked and equally well matched with a fun little medley of citrus cubes.

Out the back, with views across to the Goulburn River Valley is Herb Garden Pizzeria. The Polito wood-fire is lit from Friday to Sunday and it's a fantastic place to drop in to for a quick lunch with the family when touring the region.

There are also a number of accommodation options at Trawool Estate. The deluxe rooms are bright, luxurious and roomy, with a space for in-room dining, stunning rural views and the option of a bath. The valley rooms are well suited to families and small groups, with a kitchenette and separate bedroom with single beds.

PASSING TRAFFIC

We don't people-watch at Trawool Estate, we cyclist-watch, with just about every window of the hotel overlooking the **Great Victorian Rail Trail**. The 134km trail starts at Tallarook and ends in Mansfield, with a side-route option of ducking into Alexandra. The trail is one of Australia's longest continuous rail trails (not just for cyclists, but horse-riders and walkers too), meandering through farmland to Lake Eildon, where it starts the climb up into the Victorian High Country. A highlight is the 201m-long Cheviot Tunnel constructed to pass through the mountain range at McLoughlin's Gap, roughly halfway between Yea and Molesworth.

If you want to take a short ride from the Estate, **Yark Bikes** can deliver two-wheelers straight to the hotel, depending on availability.

WHERE WE EAT 173

#ONEHOUROUT

Greasy Zoe's

JAY DILLON

There's a story in every name. You should ask Zoe why she named the tiny eight-seater she operates with her partner Lachlan 'Greasy Zoe's'. The story is a riot, and the name is an anathema to the actual dining experience at this recently hatted little place in Hurstbridge. There's nothing dude-food, American diner or greasy about it.

Greasy Zoe's is hospitality's answer to the tiny-house movement. It's strictly a booking affair, as the eight seats fill quickly and the experience is one of being invited into Zoe and Lachlan's home. Old-school vinyl sets the scene, timber shelves against the reclaimed brick are filled with jars of ferments and there's a clear line of sight to Zoe as she creates alchemy in the kitchen. The menu is truly 'du jour'. Zoe cooks what comes in the door. There's no fussing over a long list of choices, as Zoe sets a degustation menu every night.

Many restaurants source local, but Zoe and Lachlan make you feel like you are eating and drinking the Nillumbik and Yarra Valley regions. The mushrooms and chickens are from two small-scale farms in Don Valley and the olive oil is from a small grove in Hurstbridge. One of the vegetable suppliers is from nearby St Helena where they run an on-farm training program for people with a disability.

Two local potters, Yvette De Lacy and Judy Trembath, supply plates for the table. Self-taught craftsman Eli Beke from Kinglake produces the wooden bowls and spoons, and the colourful and playful paintings that adorn the walls are by Christmas Hills artist Veronica Holland. All are made specially for Zoe and Lachlan. It's an indication of their commitment to getting it 'just right'.

Each dish requires careful consideration for what inventive amalgamation of produce and technique has occurred. Healthy, heavy mushrooms from Unearthed Mushroom Co. in Monbulk and Sugarloaf Produce in Strathewen are grilled on the wood-fire and then dressed with a chestnut paste, pickled mushrooms and a 24-hour mushroom broth. Nannygai (bight snapper) is line-caught near the continental shelf off Port Lincoln. Zoe lifts its delicate flavours by topping it with barbecued corn, shiso, basil oil and shards of its own crispy skin. You have to give it to any kitchen that makes its own cheese; at the time of writing this was a five-week wash rind–style soft cheese with milk sourced from Schultz Dairy and served with a pinwheel croissant and blood plum jelly.

Wines are matched carefully to the food. Lachlan has clearly spent time on the farms hearing the winemakers' stories. A small collection of impressive spirits adorns the top shelves behind the bar – worthy of an extra half-hour or so lingering at the table.

City slickers need not bother with the car. Head out on the Hurstbridge rail line, go to the end, and cross the road. Easy, and no designated-driver arguments.

#TWOHOURSOUT

Babil at Oddfellows

JAY DILLON

We admit to once rarely stopping for long in Colac. Most often the town served as a fuel stop whilst on the drive to the coastline west of Warrnambool or the back way into the Otway Ranges. That is until we heard news of a family-friendly Turkish restaurant opening in a 19th-century Victorian hall.

Built in 1870 to house the local branch of global philanthropic organisation, the Independent Order of Odd Fellows, (odd indeed!), the temple-like structure stands out in contrast to its neighbours. The building facade received a major makeover in 1891 to give it a rather grand classical Victorian look and includes some interesting symbolisms. Above the I.O.O.F. acronym is an open hand with a heart, symbolising charity given from the heart. The chains consisting of three links refer to the organisation's values of friendship, trust and love.

It was love too for Turkish retailer and restaurateur Serdar Basoglu when he was first shown the vacant building. Serdar previously had a Turkish restaurant near Baker Street in London's Marylebone district. After a career change into supermarkets, he ended up being sponsored by Coles to come to Australia in 2012, where he worked as regional manager, before a return to food service came calling again.

Babil at Oddfellows fills the old hall with its towering wooden ceiling. Bentwood chairs sit at bare wooden tables set with fine glassware lit by the light from large arch-shaped windows.

The menu is an eclectic mix of dishes from across Turkey. Expect to start with saganaki – a dish that's Turkish in origin. A hot slice of sheep and cow's milk cheese shallow fried and crisped on the outside and soft inside.

Move on to a dolma biber – capsicum stuffed with rice cooked with onion, garlic and tomato, redolent with cinnamon.

Always consider the mantil – Turkey's answer to ravioli. Little flat dumplings of pasta filled with minced lamb flavoured with cumin amongst other spices. It is slathered in a reduced tomato sauce seasoned with dried mint and a little whack of paprika. With walnuts for crunch and garlic yoghurt for a cooling touch, this is the go-to dish.

Look out for the small selection of Turkish wines and ask what seafood is on the menu. Come for lunch and enjoy the Turkish pop music, or at dinner the room switches to slightly more traditional Meyhane songs – folk songs performed in bars by men with smoke-cured vocal cords, lubricated by too much raki. Finish with a thick and fragrant Turkish coffee and a sugar-dusted cube of Turkish delight. Reason enough to come to Colac, we say!

VOLCANIC WONDERLAND

Roughly 12km north-west of Colac is **Red Rock Lookout**, which offers dramatic views across Lake Colac and the surrounding countryside. Visitors here are actually standing on the cone of one of Australia's youngest volcanoes and the plain before them is the third largest volcanic plain in the world.

It's quite a surreal sight with water-filled craters and sharply rising scoria cones amongst rows of stonewalls and a patchwork of paddocks managed by Western District farmers.

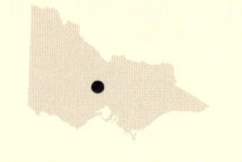

#ONEANDAHALFHOURSOUT

Bar Midland

RICHARD CORNISH

Like most people, we have a love-hate relationship with social media. Our secret hack is to never scroll. Always go in with intention. For example, checking in on what some of our favourite chefs are up to. That's how we heard about what could be the most audacious restaurant opening for years.

All meat at Bar Midland is restricted to introduced wild animals. No sugar. Just food grown around Castlemaine or harvested in Victoria, where you'll find this small bar/dining room with an almost austere Art Deco interior inside a majestic old 1870s pub.

Even the wine list is 100 per cent Victorian with wines from people like Gilles Lapalus and Simon Killeen featuring by the glass – at prices you don't need to extend your credit limit to afford. All of this comes as no surprise when you realise that conscientious chef Alex Marano is behind the 16-course menu of small plate dishes.

Every one of those dishes shouts volumes of place and season. There could be beautifully formed agnolotti filled with potato, mint and ricotta, and dressed in sharp and rich buttermilk, mandarin and fennel sauce. There are dishes cooked on the handmade charcoal grill that sits at the heart of the open kitchen, which gives the room a faint smokey tang. No beef? But there is the wild shot rabbit, slowly cooked in olive oil until it is perfect to the tooth. And do not expect salmon or barramundi – instead, order the big, meaty angasi oysters.

Marano, previously known as Alex Perry, has always been part of groundbreaking teams. He worked with Paul Mathis at the ahead-of-its-time S.O.S. (Save Our Seafood) sustainable fish restaurant in Melbourne and was part of the early MoVida team. At The Good Table in Castlemaine, he was an early adopter of the collab, bringing in chefs like Marty Beck from Dr. Marty's Crumpets to do weekly pop-ups. With fellow traveller Louden Cooper running front of house and drinks, the pair put on an incredibly disciplined service working with seasonal and local parameters.

The small dining room, part of the Midland Hotel building, is exceptionally true to the scale and ergonomics of Art Deco architects. Decorations include prints from 1930s artist (and Castlemaine woman) Christian Waller, who with husband Napier Waller designed some of Melbourne's most exceptional stained-glass windows.

For an overnight special occasion, the Midland Hotel continues with the Art Deco architecture throughout the foyer and rooms, and is handily opposite the train station.

#THREEANDAHALFHOURSOUT

Bunyip Hotel

JAY DILLON

'Is there any way we can cancel the order?'

We are standing in the kitchen of the Bunyip Hotel about to start a photoshoot and owner/chef James 'Jimmy' Campbell is on the phone to his seafood supplier. There's no stopping the seafood delivery, so instead Jimmy's focus turns to calling guests to cancel any upcoming bookings. It's heartbreaking to witness first-hand the seismic effect that the snap Covid lockdowns had on the hospitality industry. The only silver lining being the esky of King George whiting that we made the journey home with (paid for, of course).

The Bunyip Hotel is located in the middle of Cavendish, a small town tucked along the banks of the Wannon River in red gum country somewhere between Dunkeld and Balmoral. The old boozer, with Art Deco stylings, has seen many facelifts since she was built in the 1860s. Since being taken over by Campbell, the hotel has become a popular dining destination, with people driving four hours or more to dine. Jimmy is a local lad who went away to the big smoke to cook with Frank Camorra at MoVida, eventually taking the reins of the empire's Sydney restaurant. A few years back, after putting in the hard yards in the city, he returned to the family farm: a beautiful property of rolling pasture with the Gariwerd/Grampians as a dramatic backdrop. There he shored up his strength and built up his resolve. He had an idea burning inside him. He wanted to make the Bunyip great again. He knew there was enough local produce: lamb, beef, poultry, herbs, grains and vegetables. He could – and would – make a menu using food from the country around him.

Jimmy also saw the demand for good old-fashioned country cooking. 'People are over foams and that bulldust,' he says in his typical no-nonsense manner. So he took over the kitchen of the Bunyip Hotel and, eventually, the entire pub. There his photo hangs on the wall along with the other members of the Cavendish Football Club premiership team, as well as those of generations before. He polished up some old family-favourite dishes and added a few new ones. 'I couldn't have taken this on without the support of the locals,' he says. The pub is owned by several members of the community; local people helped him renovate and move into the old pub. Word got out quick and soon he was booked out on weekends. The floors are still sloping and the gents is still outside, but the food is brilliant and also reassuringly inexpensive.

In his revamped kitchen Jimmy makes aromatic black pudding served seared and hot with segments of orange and a drizzle of olive oil. His egg and chips is sensational – hand-cut Koroit spuds fried sweet and chewy, topped with an egg finished with a blowtorch and a sprinkle of smoky paprika. There's corned beef and kimchi, half poussin cooked in a soffrito with golden syrup dumplings to finish. 'It's the food I grew up on,' he says, 'with a bit of chef technique.'

WHERE WE EAT

#ONEANDAHALFHOURSOUT

Mortadeli

JAY DILLON

Chances are you'll hear Mortadeli before you see it. Classic Italian disco or '50s-style crooners always pumping loudly from the doorways of the two shopfronts that Jake Cassar operates from a courtyard just off Torquay's main drag.

Whenever we visit this little slice of Mediterranean heaven on the Surf Coast, we like to take a two-pronged approach. Firstly: we eat. Secondly: we shop.

The Deli is tiny, so the chalkboard menu, chock-full of sandwiches, is perched outside amongst the geraniums, and the seating consists of two long, wooden, communal tables that were sourced from a German beer hall and paired with little coloured stools dotted around the piazza.

Two distinct services of breakfast and lunch are split by an 11am cut-off and everything is made to order. The choices are a homage to Jake's Maltese heritage and his yearning to have been born across the water in Sicily. Each day you can expect to find flaky, golden pastizzis sitting in the pie warmer, freshly piped ricotta cannoli whispering to you from the pastry cabinet and imported soft drinks ready in

the fridge. (Hot tip: try the *Kinnie*, it's the colour of Coca-cola but with herbaceous flavours and orange undertones.)

The signature sandwich – the hobz biz-zejt – is a peasant-style offering that's been given a contemporary makeover, turning tuna and olive oil on bread into a gourmet meal the likes of which you wouldn't expect to find this side of the Equator, let alone south of Melbourne/Naarm. And just like in Italy, the coffee is top-notch, and later in the day we're always happily talked into having a spritz with our sangers.

The Grocer is the other half of Mortadeli's offering and is an immaculate rendition of an old-school European supermarket. Terrazzo flooring, colour-blocked shelves, product symmetry and mid-century style make this a feast for the eyes before anything else even registers.

This is where Jake's real talent shines because this retail arm goes so much deeper than clever visual design. He's curated and sourced a range of cheeses, cold cuts, pantry staples, fresh bread, sweets and niche smallgoods that are an absolute delight for locals and tourists.

At the time of writing, rumours have been swirling around the Surf Coast that this grocer area is to be converted into an authentic 40-seat trattoria, where guests will be able to order antipasti from the deli menu or a more hearty traditional Roma pasta dish (guanciale, Amatriciana, etc.) all made fresh on site.

As if we needed another reason to include Mortadeli on our next Surf Coast excursion.

Where we drink

It's thirsty work, this road tripping. Long days in the saddle exploring distant horizons can create a thirst like nothing else and we've been known to start happy hour just a little earlier than what's acceptable at home.

Thankfully for us, we happen to be travelling in one of the most well-stocked states on the continent and we take full advantage of this luxury.

Sometimes it's about pulling up a stool at one of the industry old-guard places, like Chambers Rosewood (*see* p. 204), who for more than 160 years has been tantalising palates with luscious wines and muscats. Then, at other times you are more likely to find us sitting in the sun with a cold cheeky rosé with some of the new generation, like at Kerri Greens (*see* p. 192).

The passion our fermenting friends show for their craft is evident wherever we go. Our state is quite often the first to launch innovations in wine, beer and spirits. And as you will see at Swiftcrest Distillery (*see* p. 197), the devotion to sustainable production practices is truly inspirational.

And it's not just all about alcohol either. Melbourne is known world-wide for its love of coffee, but you will discover through our visit to Silva Coffee (*see* p. 212) that this passion for a good brew has spread right around the state. We even have an example of a business in the north-east of Victoria bringing back old-fashioned sodas from the days of temperance (*see* p. 200) – with the option for a sneaky spicy margarita, of course!

Then when the fun is over and the moon pokes its head over the horizon, it's nice to know there are accommodation options close by. In fact, our list of pub accommodation (*see* p. 209), will often require nothing more than a climb up a timber staircase before you are tucked in bed and well-rested before another day on the road.

Let's get drinking (in moderation, of course)!

#ONEHOUROUT

Kerri Greens

JAY DILLON

The first thing you notice as you come down the gravel driveway to Kerri Greens is the expansive views across the rolling green hills north-east across the Mornington Peninsula with a gully leading down to Point Leo. The second thing are the three concrete water tanks set into the landscape and connected by a tin roof.

Quite often the best projects come about by accident. Sometimes it's just starting with a couple of mates with a shared passion, who decide to then share it with friends and family, and next thing you know there are staff, rent and all the other things that go along with a business.

Lucas Blanck is from a winemaking family in Alsace, France. He first met Tom McCarthy (from an equally well-known winemaking Mornington Peninsula wine family) whilst working harvest at Quealy Winemakers in 2010. In 2011 Tom did a vintage at Domaine Paul Blanck with Frederic Blanck (Lucas Blanck's father). This carried on until Tom became winemaker at Quealy Winemakers and Lucas was appointed viticulturist. The start of a working friendship was born and it was only a matter of time before a side project was up and about.

After a few years bringing back the health of a small, neglected block of pinot noir and pinot gris, in 2015 Tom and Lucas bottled up their first batch, selling mostly to friends and family and the odd local bottle shop. The next year they sold some more. And a few more cases the year after.

The three converted water tanks came along with the lease of The Duke Vineyard that the pair took on in 2016. The concrete was poured on-site with doors and windows cut back in after it dried. One is utilised as the cellar door, partially clad in timber strips on the outside; inside it is a bright and contemporary room with bar stools and a wine-tasting bar. The tank on the far right is a working winery and the central cylinder is the perfect for keeping past vintages cool throughout the year. In addition to serving as the barrel room, this space is also utilised for hosting workshops and exhibitions. On our visit the dynamic, thought-provoking work of painter Joshua Searle was on display.

The multipurpose barrel room is just one sign of a cellar door doing things a little differently. For a start, there are no real rules. Bring a small group or a big group, bring your dog, cat or goldfish. There are no cheese platters, small dishes or any food at all. Instead, guests are encouraged to bring their own spread and there's no shortage of farm gates around Red Hill to create an epic picnic. We were jealous though, of the clever couple who were shucking and slurping their own oysters one table over.

And why wouldn't you when you have such fantastic maritime-influenced wines on hand? The entire collection is single-vineyard wines, with their own fruit from three separate holdings, and Tom and Lucas are dedicated to organic principles at each one. Not much happens in the winery except labour, the pair preferring to let the wines develop naturally with little intervention. As a result, a tasting here is a real journey across the Mornington Peninsula landscape.

What started as two mates playing around with some spare fruit has grown into a family venture, with Tom and Lucas's partners now involved with little ones in tow too. Together they have created a fun and relaxed place to roll out a picnic rug and soak in the view across the region.

A less formal and relaxed environment that is designed for gathering is something we are seeing a lot more of as a new generation of winemakers starts opening cellar doors. You can be sure we will be seeking out more like this.

OYSTERS YOU SAY?

That's right, 150 years since almost the entire colony of native oysters was dredged from Port Phillip, they are being harvested once more. A small group of farmers are leasing sections at the southern end of the bay where they grow the same native angasi oysters that were once the staple diet of the Boon Wurrung/Bunurong and Wathaurong Peoples before Europeans arrived.

This time, instead of the oysters being gathered at low tide, they are being grown in hanging baskets just above the seafloor where they can filter the algae and microplankton brought about by the shifting tides.

You can pick up a dozen oysters for your own picnic from **Cellar and Pantry** at Red Hill.

WHERE WE DRINK

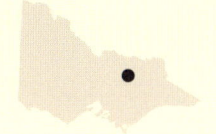

#THREEHOURSOUT

Swiftcrest Distillery

JAY DILLON

Swiftcrest Distillery champions everything good about small-batch distilling: sustainability, creativity and unhurried perfection. For Hank and Carrie Thierry, the secret to great tasting spirits is working side by side with nature through every step of the process. The couple, who opened Swiftcrest Distillery in 2019, have followed this principle to the letter. The result? A series of entirely organic, small-batch gin, vodkas and a newly released whisky to make even the toughest critic swoon.

Nestled at the foothills of the Victorian Alps in Mansfield, the location is perfect for the duo's sustainable ethos. With its cool nights and warm days, a pristine natural spring, and the fact that it was off-grid and virtually untouched, the property has allowed their dreams to become reality.

The couple's clear commitment to the environment and single-mindedness is fundamental to their approach, using biodynamic grain direct from a local farmer and making all their base spirit from scratch (98 per cent of distilleries purchase bulk spirit). A 130-year-old steam pump transports the spring water to the distillery's wood-fired steam boiler which dates back to 1906.

Naturally, fuel for the boiler is sourced from wind-felled timber across the property and solar panels provide the energy needs for the rest. To close the production circle neatly, spent grain is then fed to animals, both on and off the property.

Both Hank and Carrie have a background in fine art and photography, and their process for distilling comes together like a painting. Choices in the distillery like fermentation and mash temperatures, grain and yeast are the colour palettes they use to paint interesting and sometimes unexpected flavour profiles.

As a working farm distillery, Swiftcrest isn't the sort of venue open for the public to just drop in to. However, Hank and Carrie regularly put out dates for private tours for a maximum of 10 people (private bookings also available for up to six people). More recently, they have constructed two timber-clad tasting rooms, with floor-to-ceiling windows looking east across the Delatite valley.

The new tasting pods can be booked by groups of up to eight people which includes a menu of goods grown and grazed in the same region, which you will find stocked in the small fridges on arrival. Choices include a simple tasting plate featuring organic kalamata olives from **Strathbogie Flavours** or huge, plumb strawberries from nearby **Bimbimbi Farm**. Or for those wanting a fully cooked lunch, they can order in grass-fed organic lamb chops from **Clear Hills Lamb**, which can be cooked up with root vegetables supplied by **Heirloom Naturally**. The pods include their own two-burner barbecue, as well as glasses, cutlery and Robert Gordon crockery.

WHAT'S WITH THE NAME?

Ah, I'm glad you asked! When the couple originally purchased the property they were enamoured with the presence of swifts that migrate between Japan and Siberia and visit this part of Australia every year, appearing mostly at the top of a hill. This annual visitor was the inspiration for the name and it was the owners' talented artist daughter Belle that developed the distinctive distillery logo.

WHERE TO STAY

Swiftcrest Distillery is just 30min from Lake Eildon, so pack a tent and set up at one of the dozens of free sites around **Walsh Cove**. Here you can light a campfire at dusk and listen to the birds retire for the day. Extra points if you have a kayak.

For those of us who prefer somewhere more boutique, head to the **Alexandra Hotel** (see p.209).

#THREEHOURSOUT

Billson's Brewery and the Soda Bar

JAY DILLON

Travel surprises are the best surprises. Like when a burger joint turns out to be a hatted eight-seat restaurant (*see* Greasy Zoe's, p.174). Or an old country boozer is actually a European-inspired department store (*see* the Royal George Hotel, p.39). So, when we heard about a cocktail bar masquerading as an old-time soda cafe in Beechworth, you can be sure we were straight in the car and headed up the Hume Hwy in a flash!

Soda Bar is the latest project by Nathan and Felicity Cowan, who first arrived in town in 2017 with the ambitious project of renovating the old pigeon-filled brewery on Last St. The impressive building had a long history of relieving the thirst of the local community.

In 1865, George Billson purchased the brewery with the aim to fulfil his ambition to be a brewer (after spending time as a publican in nearby Wooragee). Outgrowing that premises, and in response to the vast requirements of a burgeoning settlement during the gold rush, George built a brew tower at the current site in Beechworth. George's brewery stayed here until the 1950s, after which it became a site for the production of cordials by Murray Breweries.

Today Billson's Brewery is brewing a growing range of quality beers, a (proper!) ginger ale, a cider and, with a clever addition to the brewery, are also distilling gin. All are excellent, and there's something for every taste. It would be remiss of us at this point to neglect to mention the basement Speakeasy bar. It's spectacular and reminiscent of the 'sly grog bars' that were the result of the temperance movement that swept through Australia in the late 19th century.

Soda Bar, located closer to the centre of Beechworth, is dedicated to this period of temperance, where the brewery handed in its alcohol licence and instead put its energies into a range of small-batch cordials, which the Cowans have lovingly

brought back to life with traditional recipes discovered as part of the renovation process. It's a small fun space, with the waiters dressed smartly in waistcoats and ties. Kids and those nostalgic for the tastes of another era can sit at the booths and enjoy sodas, spiders and mocktails. However, mention the secret password and you will be invited to somewhere where the drinks are a little more grown up!

With a flurry of communication between the waiter and a hidden figure out the back, we are motioned to enter through the door of the cool room, and, in parting the velvet curtains, Isabella's Cocktail Bar is revealed.

The room is low-lit and seductive. On the left couples huddle around small round tables and talk in whispers. It's a little more rowdy on the right with chatty blokes perched on timber bentwood stools at a black marble bar. The gents are well looked after by a capable team of bartenders slinging contemporary cocktails featuring Billson's growing list of spirits, including Isabella's namesake barrel-aged gin.

It's testament to the hidden role of women in the 19th century that only through analysing historical archives have the new owners been able to create a picture of Isabella Billson. By all accounts she was the driving force behind the couple chasing the dream of fortune in the Victorian goldfields and later in the creation of Billson's Brewery. It's never too late to bring to light forgotten or hidden characters who formed our communities.

In the kitchen is Douglas Elder, a familiar face to the One Hour Out team from heading up some of the region's most-lauded kitchens. His menu is tight and flavourful, consisting of just eight small dishes and four larger options, such as a roasted duck leg with red cabbage, mustard fruits and walnuts. To leave the bar, you must go past the kitchen to the back alley as if an act of debauchery has been committed.

So what's the password? I'm afraid the first rule of Isabella's is that you do not talk about Isabella's.

SLEEP AT BILLSON'S

For the full Billson's experience, book yourself into one of the three suites that are part of the recently renovated **The Brewer's House**. The property is just a few minutes' walk from both Soda Bar and Billson's Brewery and is the original site of the malt house that serviced the brewery. Each suite is designed with modern and clean lines; the marble-tiled bathroom is very decadent (try your best to book the deluxe suite with the bath). The garden with a solar-heated mineral water swimming pool is the place for an afternoon gin in summer.

#THREEANDAHALFHOURSOUT

Chambers Rosewood Winery

RICHARD CORNISH

The air is thick with the rich, sweet smell of ageing fortified wine. Some of it is over 130 years old. Some of it was made at the beginning of the year. It all sits under the corrugated iron of a ramshackle collection of 100-year-old white-painted sheds corralled by gnarly old peppercorns and guarded by two friendly kelpies, Jake and Leo.

The Chambers clan has been making wine here since 1858 and the latest member of the family, sixth-generation winemaker Stephen Chambers, has re-doubled his efforts into making perhaps the world's best muscat. When US wine critic Robert

Parker crowned Chambers Rare Muscat with 98/100, it became a global hit. Yet still most of the world couldn't find the rustic cellar door down a rough backroad on the outskirts of Rutherglen.

'We're still the biggest secret in Rutherglen,' says Stephen Chambers. He makes over 40 different wines and all are on tasting in the shed-like cellar door. He makes the big blokey tannin-driven durifs that Rutherglen is known for but also dabbles in the arcane French variety gouais, a light-bodied white said to be the ancestor variety of chardonnay. Wine tasting involves lining up along the hardwood bar or pulling a stool up at an old oak barrel. Before Covid you could help yourself to the wines but the 21st century – and responsible service of alcohol – caught up and now Ruth or Venetta pours the wines for you. Another recent addition is the tasting plate of local cheese and produce that you can take outside to the tables to enjoy under the old peppercorn trees.

Most people, however, come to try the muscats. These are big, super-sweet fortified wines that taste like Christmas pudding and are so beautifully crafted by blending together decades of wines stored on oak. They are made from an old French variety called muscat à petits grains rouge, which translates from the French as 'small red muscat berries'. Known locally as Rutherglen brown muscat, the grapes are allowed to fully ripen until some become raisin-like, further intensifying the flavour of the wine. The grapes are pressed, the juice partially fermented to retain the natural sugars, then the fermentation is halted by the addition of neutral alcohol. The wine is then aged in barrels, sometimes for decades in a solera system that blends old wines with young to balance fresh fruit flavours and deeper aged wines with layers of oak, oxidation and the effects of time.

'You are tasting history in every glass,' says Stephen. 'Some of the wine in our Rare Muscat was made before Australia was a nation.'

Rutherglen is known for its muscat and most wineries produce their own excellent version of this rich, luscious wine, but none have access to wines of such age stored in their own solera under a 'bloody old tin roof'.

LOOK OUT FOR CHARLIE

The Chambers's menagerie was enlarged during Covid when the two kelpies were joined by Charlie the swearing sulphur-crested cockatoo. He was excommunicated from Taronga Zoo way back in 1941 for his foul-mouthed outbursts. For the past 80 years this feathered mascot has lived in Rutherglen, formerly at Buller Wines and then at Wicked Virgin Café. Charlie's blue language has softened in his old age but occasionally he will let rip with some R-rated avine content.

MUSCAT MUSTER

Once you get bitten by the Rutherglen muscat bug you're hooked for life. It is not big business; in fact, it's an incredibly expensive wine to make as winemakers tie up thousands and thousands of litres of wine for years and years.

Near neighbours of Chambers are **Stanton & Killeen** who have an old room in the cellars, surrounded by barrels dedicated to tasting muscat. A few minutes away, overlooking a turtle-filled billabong is historic **Pfeiffer Wines** where muscat genius Jen Pfeiffer offers muscat-blending classes.

On the banks of the Murray at Wahgunya, the 19th-century castle of **All Saints Estate** has a proud new cellar door offering a high-level curated tasting of their muscats.

Out at **Scion Wine** on Slaughterhouse Rd, winemaker Rowly Milhinch is making some remarkable new wave wines whilst still being respectful to the Rutherglen muscat traditions.

Pub accommodation

RICHARD CORNISH

Once upon a time, a community couldn't call itself a town unless it had a church, a school and a pub. During the Victorian era, the fashion was to build grand buildings with large dining rooms to feed travellers during the day and evening and then accommodate them in rooms at night.

The countryside is dotted with these beautiful old boozers. Some are falling into ruin, some are now private homes while, thankfully, some still offer excellent meals and stylish surrounds for a comfortable stay. Here are four of Victoria's best old pubs with great food and good rooms.

#TWOHOURSOUT

The Alexandra Hotel
Alexandra

The Alexandra Hotel sits in the heart of the beautiful little town of Alexandra, 70km north of Healesville, just west of Lake Eildon. This classic old pub was built in 1903 in the late Victorian style and was given a lot of love and a sympathetic makeover in recent years. For some, it's the night's stop after a hard day on the Great Victorian Rail Trail, but for us, and an increasing number of food lovers, the pub's a destination in itself.

Co-owner and head chef is Patrick Browning, formerly with the Melbourne Wine Room under Karen Martini. He takes local produce and turns it into satisfying dishes such as house-smoked pumpkin served on his own sourdough with poached eggs, cashews, avocado and dukkah for the weekend brunch menu.

We recommend grabbing a table by the fire, taking a seat in the upholstered carved chairs and getting head down into some Loddon Estate free-range chicken with potato and pancetta terrine or an 800g chargrilled Sabre Pastoral grass-fed ribeye. There's a beautiful wine list supporting many local wineries. With superb countryside nearby, it's worth booking one of the well-appointed ensuite bedrooms with views out over the balcony and the bustling township below for a weekend in the country.

#ONEANDAHALFHOURSOUT

Harvest Home
Avenel

When Ned Kelly was a boy, he saved the life of another lad from drowning in Hughes Creek on the outskirts of his hometown called Avenel, just north of Seymour. It's a beautiful historic little town with one of the state's best butcher shops – **Avenel Meats** – and a swathe of wineries nearby in Nagambie and the

Strathbogie Ranges. The train running from Southern Cross in Melbourne/Naarm to Wodonga pulls in several times a day to the station, a short walk to the 1870 Harvest Home.

With its broad verandahs, wine cellar and semicircular brass-topped bar, this old boozer is now a boutique hotel and restaurant. The six rooms upstairs offer charming old-world accommodation with antique chairs and sideboards paired with plush bed linen, charming ensuites, and heating and cooling. The dining room captures the height of Victorian pomp with carved ladder-backed and balloon-backed chairs, parlour plants and open fireplaces.

Outside in the large sprawling garden are fun, funky bohemian and chic dining spaces and towering trees. Chef Martin Golding makes the most of his kitchen garden in dishes like twice-baked gruyère souffle with freshly picked garden salad and potato and leek soup. While the eye fillet is great, it is the mashed potato with two-day reduced jus that's our reason to drive up the Hume Hwy. Together with dishes like confit duck and roast chicken with Israeli couscous, and a focus on regional wines, the Harvest Home has become a popular destination for couples and friends to come for the weekend.

#THREEHOURSOUT
Criterion Hotel
Sale

This part of Gippsland, between 90 Mile Beach, the Macalister and Thomson rivers and ranges beyond, is becoming very popular with fishers, hunters and bike riders. For us, one of the main attractions is the ever-changing calendar of exhibitions at **Gippsland Art Gallery** in Sale. A good hub is the Criterion Hotel on Macalister St, a historic pub making a name for its great grub – and with boutique rooms.

Built in the 1880s, the Criterion has been given a modern, rustic makeover that blends fencing-wire lampshades with faux-library wallpaper and clean white lines in the main dining room. The food is a good step up from pub grub steering into gastro-pub turf with starters such as a soft, sweet, sticky, peanuty eggplant bao or a plate of fried tiny baby squid with a good dollop of aioli and fresh sharp chimichurri. However, you will find us waddling back to our room after ordering the 350g free-range Gippsland porterhouse with jus, salad and fries or a fat, juicy chicken schnitzel topped with napoli sauce and tangy Maffra cheddar.

Upstairs the rooms are spacious, modern, and well appointed, each with its own ensuite. Some look out onto the iron lacework of the balcony and beyond. Being in the heart of town, we find it an excellent point to kick off an exploration of this beautiful region.

#FOURHOURSOUT
Royal Hotel, Sea Lake
Sea Lake

For years a stream of tourists has headed up the Calder Hwy to catch the elusive beauty of the salt-encrusted surface of Lake Tyrell in northern Victoria. The problem was that there was nowhere to stay after the 4hr drive from Melbourne/Naarm. Then, a few years back, a group of 17 local farmers and business people pooled their cash and bought the then-closed Royal Hotel at nearby Sea Lake for just $180,000. This beautiful two-storey pub with wrap-around verandah was built in 1910 in the late Victorian style. The consortium poured a motzah into the old boozer. They gave it a new bar, outdoor area and a flash new dining room.

There are now 17 newly refurbished bedrooms, some pet friendly. The upstairs bedrooms have access to the balcony, which faces north-west and has magnificent views of the sunset over town. The Juke is the pub's dining room, a lease agreement with restaurateurs Ezra Tepania and Dylan Walsh who concentrate on local produce to service their upmarket bistro menu. The combination of drinking with the locals in a historic pub, views of nearby Lake Tyrell and really good pub grub makes the Royal a no-brainer for us.

LEFT, OPPOSITE TOP AND PREVIOUS Criterion Hotel
OPPOSITE BOTTOM LEFT AND RIGHT Harvest Home

WHERE WE DRINK

#ONEANDAHALFHOURSOUT

Silva Coffee

JAY DILLON

When Cleo and Wayne Silva began importing and roasting coffee in a Wesburn warehouse in 2016, their mission from the very beginning was to educate coffee drinkers in what elements need to come together to create the perfect cup. In homage to the many cellar doors in the Yarra Valley, they opened a 'roastery door' where visitors could come and see the beans being roasted, learn about the farmers who grow the product and experience the flavours that come from single-origin and unique blends.

This mission was further extended at the end of the Covid lockdowns, when the couple opened a 'coffee tasting bar' beside the waterwheel of their hometown of Warburton. It's a beautiful location on the high side of the street, shaded by a large elm tree and with views back towards Mt Donna Buang.

'So what exactly is a coffee tasting bar?' I hear you ask. Well, Cleo and Wayne are convinced that the nuances and complexity present in a fresh brew should be treated equally to an aromatic gin or a barrel-aged shiraz. And why not, when the key flavour factors for coffee of 'geography, variety, processing and roasting' are mostly familiar to any wine drinker (thankfully, we have never heard of anyone roasting grapes).

There are three different coffee flights to choose from the menu. The Espresso flight is served without milk and is likely the way to achieve the most honest expression of flavours across the four samples. The Piccolo flight is the milk (or alternative milk) version and the Trio flight is a mix of filter, espresso and piccolo. We love that they provide a flavour wheel with the flight and the barista encourages us to use the wheel to seek out varying levels of flavours in categories like sweet, green, spices and floral.

Each coffee comes with a card that includes tasting notes and origin information. Here we learn that the cold brew sample, with flavours of light berry fruitiness, is from a co-operative farming community about 150km north of Nairobi, Kenya. This is in complete contrast to Bom Jesus, a smooth, hazelnut latte farmed by a husband-and-wife team in the Alta Mogiana region north of São Paulo, Brazil. The next coffee, served black, is farmed by the Yirgacheffe Coffee Farmers Union in the Gedo region of Southern Ethiopia. It's one of our favourites, with a smooth buttery texture and notes of chocolate and vanilla.

The last coffee on the flight isn't a coffee at all. It's a tea or tisane, made from coffee bean husk steeped in hot water. The Spanish word for this is 'cascara', where the coffee cherry is collected after processing and dried in the sun. The husk in this case originates from Honduras and creates a refreshing tea with hints of apple and raisins. 'Coffee tea' is a confusing concept, although we love hearing about any time a waste product from any process is utilised to its full potential.

Throughout this journey of coffee discovery, the small-batch roaster is whirring away in the background. Locals and visitors alike drop in to restock their home supply of beans or stop for a single-origin brew the way they like it. Cleo and Wayne are on a mission to change people's perceptions of coffee and bring it more into line with the reverence given to other drops the Yarra Valley is famous for.

More places to bean seen

#ONEHOUROUT
Cartel Roasters
Geelong

Should one wake up with a hangover in Geelong, as one often does, then one heads directly to Coffee Cartel on Little Malop St. It's a small space with a large communal table that serves as a great location to watch pilgrims enter to worship at the altar of Slayer. If you really want to start exploring the world of single-origin coffee and specialty teas, this is a great place to start. We prefer a slower start to the day with a long black and bagel ruben.

At the end of the Covid lockdowns the Cartel team opened a stylish wine and cocktail bar next door with the same dedication to refined quality.

#ONEANDAHALFHOURSOUT
Ocean Grind
Torquay

The laid-back and sustainable ethos of the Surf Coast flows into all aspects of Ocean Grind's coffee roastery in Torquay. From the careful selection of ethical coffee farms around the globe to the slow and small-batch roasting that takes place in their Torquay home, this crew puts as much love into coffee as they do into surfing – and that's saying something. These beans are widely distributed across the Surf Coast; we recommend giving their flagship cafe a visit, but remember to bring your reusable cup! No single-use cups are in sight here.

#ONEHOUROUT
Coffee Basics
Castlemaine

Traditional European coffee craftsmanship meets central Victorian standards at the Coffee Basics Rösterei and cafe Das Kaffeehaus in Castlemaine. Helmed by Edmund Schaerf and Elna Schaerf-Trauner, Coffee Basics is the result of 60 years of family tradition in the roasting and blending business. Their small-batch, artisan coffee beans come in either single-origin or blend packs and can be ordered online.

#ONEHOUROUT
Martin St Coffee Roasters
Blackwood

They say the air is pure around the forested hills of Blackwood. The founder duo of Martin St Coffee take full advantage of this by air roasting small quantities of sustainably sourced beans. Fluid-bed air-roasters (in contrast to conventional drum roasters) only use air to roast the beans, which provides precise control and complexity of flavours.

These guys are serious coffee nuts and, although it's not really a traditional type of cafe experience, you can drop by on most mornings for a look around their workshop, sample their products, cosy up for a coffee or grab a takeaway.

#TWOANDAHALFHOURSOUT
Mansfield Coffee Merchant
Mansfield

This is specialty coffee that has caught the eye of some of Melbourne's toughest coffee critics. Mansfield Coffee Merchant burst onto the scene in 2014 and has turned the sleepy High Country town into an industry leader. They roast their single-origin coffee and signature blends on-site, package them in compostable packaging and sell them direct to the public. Plus, they even have Nespresso-compatible coffee pods. What more could you want?

Index

A
Ada Tree 157–8
Agnes Falls 19
Alexandra 172, 209
Alexandra Hotel 199, 209
Allans Flat Reserve 9
Anglesea 145
Anglesea Heath 139, 145–6
anti-gravity hill 105
Apollo Bay 74
Apollo Bay Fisherman's Co-op 74
Arrow Fisheries 74
Arthurs Seat 19
Artisan Village 59
Australian Botanic Gardens 119, 148–9
Australian Pinball Museum 112–15
Avenel 209–10
Avenel Meats 209

B
Babil at Oddfellows 177–9
Bairnsdale 168
bakeries 81–3
Ballarat 9, 50, 52–5, 84, 139, 157
Ballarat's Avenue of Honour 157
Balmoral 184
banksia forests 147
Bar Midland 180–1
Barwon Heads 49
Bass and Flinders Distillery 43
beaches 16
Beechworth 46–7, 131, 200–3
Beechworth Conservatory 46–7
Benalla 4, 7
Benalla Art Gallery 7
Bendigo 50, 56–9
Bendigo Antiques and Collectibles Centre 56–8
Bendigo Book Mark 50
Bendigo Ernest Hotel 59
Bendigo Pottery 57, 59
Big Tree, The 158
Billson's Brewery 200, 203
Bimbimbi Farm 198
Black Barn Farm 77–8
Blackwood 22–3, 215
Blackwood Distillery 37
Blackwood Mineral Springs 22–3
Blackwood Mineral Springs Caravan Park 23
Blue Pool 10
Boandik People 27
Boatshed Cheese 43
Book Bind, The 50
Bookgrove 49
Bookshop at Queenscliff, The 49
bookshops 49–51
Boom Gallery 109–11
Boon Wurrung/Bunurong People 19, 70, 157, 195
Boort 158

Box Office 111
Brewer's House, The 203
Briagalong 10
Bright 9, 50
Bright Bookshop, The 50
Brother Lawrence 109
Budj Bim Cultural Landscape 161–3
Bunyip, The 20
Bunyip Hotel 183–5
Buxton Trout and Salmon Farm 74

C
Cabbage Tree Creek 146
cabbage trees 146–7
Cabosse & Feve 68
Calembeen Park 10
Cape Conran 147
Cape Paterson 9, 79
Cape Paterson Bay 9
Cape Schanck 14
Cartel Roasters 215
Casterton 20
Castlemaine 9, 67–9, 82, 158, 180–1, 215
Castlemaine Central Wine Store 69
Cavendish 20, 183–5
Cellar and Pantry 195
Centenary Park 9
Chambers Rosewood Winery 204–7
Childers Cove 16

Chojo Feature Trees Gallery and
    Nursery 106–7
Clear Hills Lamb 198
Cobram 16
Coffee Basics 215
Colac 177–9
Corroboree Tree 157
Creswick 10, 82, 139
Criterion Hotel 210
Croajingolong National Park 147

D

Dandenong Ranges 106–7, 146
Dartmoor 27, 28
Daylesford 9, 19, 79, 87–9, 158
Daylesford Longhouse 87–9
Den of Nargun 10, 20
Dhudhuroa People 130
Diamond Bay 13–15
Dixon's Creek 90–3
Dja Dja Wurrung People 158
Dromana 42–5
Dromana Habitat 42–4
Dunkeld 20, 183

E

Edible Forest 90–3
Eldorado Road 47
English oak 158
Errinundra Plateau 145
Everwhere Denim 43

F

Fairy Cove 16
FarmacyCo 47
Feather & Drum Custom Hat Co.
    34–7
Fin Wines 93
First Nations People 4–7, 19, 20, 27,
    64–5, 70, 115, 130, 139, 140–1, 143,
    146–7, 157, 161–3

Flats, The, Mooroopna 140–1
Flinders 70–3, 154–5
Flinders Mussels 70–3, 155
Flinders Pier 154–5
forests 145–7
Fresh Fish on Pascoe 74

G

Gardens of St Erth 23
Gariwerd/Grampians 20, 27, 139
Gawa Wurundjeri Resource Trail
    64–5
Geelong 50, 109–11, 215
Geelong Fresh Foods 111
Gippsland Art Gallery 210
Glenylon General Store 19
Goshen Country 79
Graze 74
Greasy Zoe's 174–5, 200
Great Ocean Road 139
Great Ocean Troves, The 50
Great Victorian Rail Trial 172
Guard, The 37
Guildford 158
Guildford Family Hotel 158
Gunai/Kurnai People 20, 143
Gunditjmara People 20, 27, 161–3

H

Hall's Gap 139
Happy Baker 37
Harcourt 68
Harvest Home 209
Hastings 156
Hattah-Kulkyne National Park 151–3
Hawthorn 157
Heads and Tales Bookstore 49
Healesville 49, 143
Healesville Sanctuary 143
Heirloom Naturally 198
Henry of Harcourt 69

Hepburn Springs 89
Heywood 161
Hotel Vera 55
Hurstbridge 174–5

I

Inglenook Dairy 84–5
Inglewood 59
Ink Bookshop 50

J

Jean-Claude Van on a Dam 55
Jenkins & Sons Fresh Fish 74
Jetty Road 43
JimmyRum Distillery 43
Johnny Alloo 55
Johnny Baker 82
Jonai Farms and Meatsmiths 79

K

Kerri Greens (winery) 192–5
Ket Baker 82
Kings Falls 19
Kiosk, The 29
Known World, The 50
Kyneton 39–41, 98–101, 127–9
Kyneton Community Park 40
Kyneton Springs Motel 128

L

La Conchilia food van 70, 155
Ladies Bath Falls 9–10
Lake Condah 161, 162
Lake Esmond 9
Lakes Entrance 74
Latje Latje People 151
Le Péché Gourmand 82
leadbeater's possum (Wollert) 142–3
LEFCOL 74
Lindenow 20, 168–9
Little Desert National Park 115

Little Rebel 43
Loddon Falls 19
Long Paddock, The 20, 168-9
Long Paddock Cheese 67-9
Lorne 50, 146
Lorne Books 50
Lower Glenelg River 25-8
Lyons Will Estate 101

M

Macedon Ranges 98-105
Maldon 82
Maldon Bakery 82
Mallacoota 147
mangrove forests 146
Mansfield 50, 172, 197-9, 215
Mansfield Coffee Merchant 215
Marlo 147
Martin St Coffee Roasters 215
Mildura 151
Miller's Bread Kitchen 45
Mitchell River National Park 20
Molesworth 172
Mooroopna 140-1
Mornington Peninsula 13-14, 19, 42-5, 70-3, 146, 154-5, 192-4
Mortadeli 186-7
Mount Buffalo National Park 9-10
Mount Monument 102-5
Mount Pilot 130
mountain ash forests 146
MOVE 119, 123-5
MP Cheese Merchants 43
Mr Mussels 74
Murnane Bay 16
Murray River beaches 16
Murrnong Farm 79

N

Nagambie 209
Need2Read 50

Nelson 27, 28, 29
Nelson Hotel 29
Nhill 112-15, 147
Nigretta Falls 20
Nillumbik Estate 65

O

Oakwood Smallgoods 68
Oasis Motel 115
Ocean Grind 215
Ocean Grove 49
on Country (First Nations) 139, 140-1
Orbost 145
Otway Ranges 146
Ouyen 147
Ox and Hound Bistro, The 47

P

Palais 89
Pallanganmiddang Country 77
Panton Hill Bushland Reserve System 65
Pastoria East 98
Peninsula Fresh Seafood 3
Peony & Weasel Flower Co 111
Pete Deegan's fish shop 74
Peterborough 16
Pfeiffer Wines 207
Phillip Island 50
pom-me-granite 98-101
Port Fairy 161
Portarlington 74
Portarlington Grand Hotel 74
Portarlington Mussel Tours 74
Portland 74
Powelltown 157
Project 49 47

Q

Queenscliff 49

R

Ragazzone 55
Red Hill 192-5
Red Hill Candle Co. 43
Red Rock Lookout 178
Rhino Tiger Bear 43
river red gum 157
Romsey 102-5
Rosehaven Farm 79
Rossco's 111
Royal George Hotel 39-41, 200
Royal Hotel, Sea Lake 210
Rutherglen 204-7

S

St Kilda 157
Sale 210
San Remo 74
San Remo Fisherman's Co-op 74
Sandy Cove 16
Sassafras 106-7
Scar Tree, Boort 158
Scion Wine 207
Sea Bounty Mussels 74
Sea Lake 210
Seawinds Gardens 19
Secret Garden Gigs 120-1
Settler & Sons 55
Seymour 171, 172
Shepparton 82, 117-19, 123-5, 148-9
Shepparton Art Museum (SAM) 117-19
significant trees 157-9
Silva Coffee 90, 212-13
Slatey Creek 139
Smiths Gully Cafe 65
Soda Bar 200-3
Sorrento 13-15
Sprout Bakery 68
Stanley 77-8
Stanton & Killeen 207

Stockroom 127–9
Strathbogie Flavours 198
Strathmerton 16
Strzelecki Ranges 146
Swiftcrest Distillery 197–9
swimming holes 8–11

T

Tallarook 171, 172
Tatura 120–1
Taungurung People/Country 98, 141
The Big Tree 158
The Book Bind 50
The Bookshop at Queenscliff 49
The Brewer's House 203
The Bright Bookshop 50
The Bunyip 20
The Flats, Mooroopna 140–1
The Great Ocean Troves 50
The Guard 37
The Kiosk 29
The Known World 50
The Long Paddock 20, 168–9
The Ox and Hound Bistro 47
The Vegan Dairy 43
Tinto 82
Tiny 47
Tocumwal 16
Toora 19–20

Torquay 50, 186–7, 215
Torquay Books 50
Tower Hill 139
Trawool 171–3
Trawool Estate 171–3
trees, significant 157–9
Tulip 111
Turn the Page Bookshop 50

U

Ulupna Island 16

V

Valencia Creek 136–7
Vaughan Springs 9, 158
Vegan Dairy, The 43
Verdant Dwellings 43
Verso Books 49
Village Café and Wine Bar 73
Violet Town 79

W

Walsh Cove 199
Wangaratta 4
Wannon Falls 20
Warburton 212–13
Warragul 50
Wartook Valley 79
waterfalls 19–21

Watsons Creek 64–5
weedy sea dragons 154–5
Wellington 82
Western Port 146, 154
wildflowers 136–9, 145–6
Wilson's Promontory 16
Windflower 52–5
Winnap 28
Winton Wetlands 4–7
Wonthaggi 79
Woowookarung Regional Park 139
Wotjobaluk People 27, 115
Wurundjeri People 64–5, 143, 157
Wyperfeld National Park 147

Y

Yackandandah 9, 34–7
Yark Bikes 172
Yarra Glen 93
Yarra Ranges National Park 142–3
Yarra Valley 49, 64, 90–3, 212–13
Yarrawonga 16
Yea 171, 172
Yeddonba Aboriginal Cultural Site 130
Yorta Yorta People/Country 4–7, 117, 140–1, 149

Acknowledgements

If it takes a village to raise a child, then it takes a small army to get a book out into the world. And I am eternally grateful for the battalion of talented people who put their hearts and minds into the task of bringing to life the book that you now hold in your hands.

To my dear friend Richard Cornish. If there was a lifetime achievement award for contributions to Victoria's regional communities, then you are the only possible candidate. Likewise, myself and One Hour Out have been a constant benefactor of your seemingly endless generosity, deep wisdom and deft talent with the written word. I look forward to more walks together.

To Della Vreeland, thank you for your beautifully crafted words and unwavering commitment to this project. I am constantly amazed by your ability to creatively capture the essence of a location or the character of a person. Sometimes I just needed to hear your infectious laughter in order to be propelled past another seemingly insurmountable hill.

A big shout out to the many gifted local photographers whose contributions brought the words to life with their astonishing ability to shape and capture light. With a very special mention to Mike Emmett, who was not only the founding photographer for OHO, but through the years of sharing long-drives, fast-paced photoshoots, compact motel rooms and late-night eats in tiny country towns; became confidante, counsellor and friend. Thanks for everything Mike, you are a truly gifted and generous soul.

On reflection, it's possible I underestimated the workload required for a project like this and I am eternally grateful to Faye McCormack for stepping up and taking the reins of One Hour Out during my long periods of absence. Faye has been with One Hour Out from the very beginning and is the ever-reliable engine that has kept things going over the years and someone I'm honoured to work alongside of. Thank you for everything Faye.

This book would be nothing more than a shower-thought without the talented team at Hardie Grant Explore, who possess a deep passion for travel and the skills and patience for giving a voice to new authors like team OHO. Thank you first to Melissa Kayser for believing in our team in the first place. You had a vision and we are grateful that you entrusted us with the task of making it real. To the wonderful Megan Cuthbert, for keeping everything and everyone focused and on track and instilling in our team the confidence to keep forging ahead. To the copy-editing powerhouse Alice Barker, thank you for your diligence, eye for detail and bringing our ramblings into line. Thank you too, to Susan Keogh for bringing your eagle eye to the final pages and to Simone Wall for taking this jumble of letters and photos right through to a real-life book. We are also grateful to Jamil Tye, First Nations consultant and Yorta Yorta man, whose deep knowledge of Victoria's First Nations culture guided us throughout.

Part of our enthusiasm for taking on this project was the comfort of knowing such a masterful team was tasked with creating a book that was visually beautiful and that could sit proudly alongside the many other books that we admire in the Hardie Grant Explore catalogue. My most heart-felt gratitude goes to Susanne Geppert for layout and typesetting, the beautiful cartography work of Emily Maffei and all the wonderfully talented people at Evi-O.Studios.

To all the dedicated members of Victoria's vibrant tourism and hospitality industry. It's been a tough few years, probably the hardest that any generation has had to face. The OHO team and I are constantly amazed and humbled at your ability to continue to welcome us (and all your visitors) with an open door and a warm bed throughout. Victoria is certainly blessed with stunning natural beauty, but it's the people that make it one of the world's great destinations.

Lastly, allow me to indulge in acknowledging the love and support from my two incredible children, Bonnie and Vincent, who are my constant source of inspiration, my co-parent Rachael Rose, my ever-loving parents, John and Joy, and my best mates posing as brothers, Kelly and Wade.

Jay Dillon
Founder – One Hour Out

Photography credits

All images © Jay Dillon, with the exception of the following:

Front cover: Paige Shott; Back cover: Windflower

Pages 10, 47, 190, 212, 213, 214 Hugh Davidson; xv, xvi (bottom), 50, 51, 65, 75 (bottom right), 107, 141, 148, 149, 170, 171, 173, 208, 210, 211 (top) Mike Emmett; xvi (top), 18, 62, 76, 77, 78, 79, 131, 186, 187 Nicky Cawood; 2, 12, 14, 15, 42, 44, 45, 71, 72, 73, 192, 193, 194 Chris McConville; 22 Samin Todd; 31, 54, 55 Jessica Tremp; 32, 38, 41 Tara Pearce; 53 Dan Roberts; 61, 90, 91, 92 A Myszka; 76, 77, 78, 79, 131 Bec Haycraft; 66, 67, 68, 69 Angelica James; 86, 87, 88, 89 Phillip Huynh; 95, 118 (top) Leon Schoots; 96, 122, 124, 125 MOVE; 108, 110, 111 Carli Wilson; 116 Cam Matheson; 118 (bottom) Christian Capurro; 119 John Gollings; 121 Lingy Harhangy Photography; 126, 128, 129 Q1 Choi; 133, 150, 152, 153 Michael Rolph; 137 (top) Shutterstock; 151 Scott Rolph; 137 (bottom), 138 Visit Victoria; 142, 154, 155 Alamy; 160, 161, 163 Budj Bim Cultural Landscape Tourism; 174, 175 Kristoffer Paulsent; 178 Lauren Doolan; 181 Tim Grey; 182, 183, 185 Bunyip Hotel; 196 Rob Blackburn; 197, 199 Tasha Tylee; 198 Hank Thierry; 189, 201, 202 Erin Davis Hartwig: 206 (left) Sue Davis.

Published in 2023 by Hardie Grant Explore,
an imprint of Hardie Grant Publishing

Hardie Grant Explore (Melbourne)
Wurundjeri Country
Building 1, 658 Church Street
Richmond, Victoria 3121

Hardie Grant Explore (Sydney)
Gadigal Country
Level 7, 45 Jones Street
Ultimo, NSW 2007

www.hardiegrant.com/au/explore

All rights reserved. No part of this publication may be reproduced, stored in a retrieval system or transmitted in any form by any means, electronic, mechanical, photocopying, recording or otherwise, without the prior written permission of the publishers and copyright holders.

The moral rights of the author have been asserted.

Copyright text © One Hour Out 2023
Copyright concept, maps and design © Hardie Grant Publishing 2023

The maps in this publication incorporate data from © Commonwealth of Australia (Geoscience Australia), 2006. Geoscience Australia has not evaluated the data as altered and incorporated within this publication, and therefore gives no warranty regarding accuracy, completeness, currency or suitability for any particular purpose.

 A catalogue record for this book is available from the National Library of Australia

Hardie Grant acknowledges the Traditional Owners of the Country on which we work, the Wurundjeri People of the Kulin Nation and the Gadigal People of the Eora Nation, and recognises their continuing connection to the land, waters and culture. We pay our respects to their Elders past and present.

For all relevant publications, Hardie Grant Explore commissions a First Nations consultant to review relevant content and provide feedback to ensure suitable language and information is included in the final book. Hardie Grant Explore also includes traditional place names and acknowledges Traditional Owners, where possible, in both the text and mapping for their publications.

Undiscovered Victoria
ISBN 9781741178807

10 9 8 7 6 5 4 3 2 1

Publisher Melissa Kayser
Project editor Megan Cuthbert
Editor Alice Barker
Proofreader Susan Keogh
First Nations consultant Jamil Tye, Yorta Yorta
Cartographer Emily Maffei
Design Evi-O.Studios | Katherine Zhang
Typesetting Susanne Geppert
Index Max McMaster
Production coordinator Simone Wall

Colour reproduction by Simone Wall and Splitting Image Colour Studio

Printed and bound in China by LEO Paper Products LTD.

 The paper this book is printed on is certified against the Forest Stewardship Council® Standards and other sources. FSC® promotes environmentally responsible, socially beneficial and economically viable management of the world's forests.

Disclaimer: While every care is taken to ensure the accuracy of the data within this product, the owners of the data (including the state, territory and Commonwealth governments of Australia) do not make any representations or warranties about its accuracy, reliability, completeness or suitability for any particular purpose and, to the extent permitted by law, the owners of the data disclaim all responsibility and all liability (including without limitation, liability in negligence) for all expenses, losses, damages (including indirect or consequential damages) and costs which might be incurred as a result of the data being inaccurate or incomplete in any way and for any reason.

Publisher's Disclaimers: The publisher cannot accept responsibility for any errors or omissions. The representation on the maps of any road or track is not necessarily evidence of public right of way. The publisher cannot be held responsible for any injury, loss or damage incurred during travel. It is vital to research any proposed trip thoroughly and seek the advice of relevant state and travel organisations before you leave.

Publisher's Note: Every effort has been made to ensure that the information in this book is accurate at the time of going to press. The publisher welcomes information and suggestions for correction or improvement.